C-2630   CAREER EXAMINATION SERIES

This is your
PASSBOOK for...

Supervising Medical Social Worker

Test Preparation Study Guide
Questions & Answers

COPYRIGHT NOTICE

This book is SOLELY intended for, is sold ONLY to, and its use is RESTRICTED to individual, bona fide applicants or candidates who qualify by virtue of having seriously filed applications for appropriate license, certificate, professional and/or promotional advancement, higher school matriculation, scholarship, or other legitimate requirements of education and/or governmental authorities.

This book is NOT intended for use, class instruction, tutoring, training, duplication, copying, reprinting, excerption, or adaptation, etc., by:

1) Other publishers
2) Proprietors and/or Instructors of "Coaching" and/or Preparatory Courses
3) Personnel and/or Training Divisions of commercial, industrial, and governmental organizations
4) Schools, colleges, or universities and/or their departments and staffs, including teachers and other personnel
5) Testing Agencies or Bureaus
6) Study groups which seek by the purchase of a single volume to copy and/or duplicate and/or adapt this material for use by the group as a whole without having purchased individual volumes for each of the members of the group
7) Et al.

Such persons would be in violation of appropriate Federal and State statutes.

PROVISION OF LICENSING AGREEMENTS – Recognized educational, commercial, industrial, and governmental institutions and organizations, and others legitimately engaged in educational pursuits, including training, testing, and measurement activities, may address request for a licensing agreement to the copyright owners, who will determine whether, and under what conditions, including fees and charges, the materials in this book may be used them. In other words, a licensing facility exists for the legitimate use of the material in this book on other than an individual basis. However, it is asseverated and affirmed here that the material in this book CANNOT be used without the receipt of the express permission of such a licensing agreement from the Publishers. Inquiries re licensing should be addressed to the company, attention rights and permissions department.

All rights reserved, including the right of reproduction in whole or in part, in any form or by any means, electronic or mechanical, including photocopying, recording, or by any information storage and retrieval system, without permission in writing from the Publisher.

Copyright © 2025 by
National Learning Corporation

212 Michael Drive, Syosset, NY 11791
(516) 921-8888 • www.passbooks.com
E-mail: info@passbooks.com

PASSBOOK® SERIES

THE *PASSBOOK® SERIES* has been created to prepare applicants and candidates for the ultimate academic battlefield – the examination room.

At some time in our lives, each and every one of us may be required to take an examination – for validation, matriculation, admission, qualification, registration, certification, or licensure.

Based on the assumption that every applicant or candidate has met the basic formal educational standards, has taken the required number of courses, and read the necessary texts, the *PASSBOOK® SERIES* furnishes the one special preparation which may assure passing with confidence, instead of failing with insecurity. Examination questions – together with answers – are furnished as the basic vehicle for study so that the mysteries of the examination and its compounding difficulties may be eliminated or diminished by a sure method.

This book is meant to help you pass your examination provided that you qualify and are serious in your objective.

The entire field is reviewed through the huge store of content information which is succinctly presented through a provocative and challenging approach – the question-and-answer method.

A climate of success is established by furnishing the correct answers at the end of each test.

You soon learn to recognize types of questions, forms of questions, and patterns of questioning. You may even begin to anticipate expected outcomes.

You perceive that many questions are repeated or adapted so that you can gain acute insights, which may enable you to score many sure points.

You learn how to confront new questions, or types of questions, and to attack them confidently and work out the correct answers.

You note objectives and emphases, and recognize pitfalls and dangers, so that you may make positive educational adjustments.

Moreover, you are kept fully informed in relation to new concepts, methods, practices, and directions in the field.

You discover that you are actually taking the examination all the time: you are preparing for the examination by "taking" an examination, not by reading extraneous and/or supererogatory textbooks.

In short, this PASSBOOK®, used directedly, should be an important factor in helping you to pass your test.

SUPERVISING MEDICAL SOCIAL WORKER

DUTIES
Performs professional medical social work and supervises medical social workers consulting on medical-social aspects of casework. An employee in this class supervises the social work services of a health center, or a major medical or mental health social work program. Work is primarily administrative in nature and includes development and implementation of program goals, budget preparation, writing grant proposals and supervision of professional, paraprofessional and clerical staff. The incumbent exercises a considerable degree of independent judgment and initiative. Performs related work as required.

SCOPE OF THE EXAMINATION
The written test will cover knowledge, skills and/or abilities in such areas as:

1. Principles and practices of medical social work;
2. Administration;
3. Supervision;
4. Understanding and interpreting written material;
5. Preparing written material; and
6. Medical terminology.

HOW TO TAKE A TEST

I. YOU MUST PASS AN EXAMINATION

A. *WHAT EVERY CANDIDATE SHOULD KNOW*

Examination applicants often ask us for help in preparing for the written test. What can I study in advance? What kinds of questions will be asked? How will the test be given? How will the papers be graded?

As an applicant for a civil service examination, you may be wondering about some of these things. Our purpose here is to suggest effective methods of advance study and to describe civil service examinations.

Your chances for success on this examination can be increased if you know how to prepare. Those "pre-examination jitters" can be reduced if you know what to expect. You can even experience an adventure in good citizenship if you know why civil service exams are given.

B. *WHY ARE CIVIL SERVICE EXAMINATIONS GIVEN?*

Civil service examinations are important to you in two ways. As a citizen, you want public jobs filled by employees who know how to do their work. As a job seeker, you want a fair chance to compete for that job on an equal footing with other candidates. The best-known means of accomplishing this two-fold goal is the competitive examination.

Exams are widely publicized throughout the nation. They may be administered for jobs in federal, state, city, municipal, town or village governments or agencies.

Any citizen may apply, with some limitations, such as the age or residence of applicants. Your experience and education may be reviewed to see whether you meet the requirements for the particular examination. When these requirements exist, they are reasonable and applied consistently to all applicants. Thus, a competitive examination may cause you some uneasiness now, but it is your privilege and safeguard.

C. *HOW ARE CIVIL SERVICE EXAMS DEVELOPED?*

Examinations are carefully written by trained technicians who are specialists in the field known as "psychological measurement," in consultation with recognized authorities in the field of work that the test will cover. These experts recommend the subject matter areas or skills to be tested; only those knowledges or skills important to your success on the job are included. The most reliable books and source materials available are used as references. Together, the experts and technicians judge the difficulty level of the questions.

Test technicians know how to phrase questions so that the problem is clearly stated. Their ethics do not permit "trick" or "catch" questions. Questions may have been tried out on sample groups, or subjected to statistical analysis, to determine their usefulness.

Written tests are often used in combination with performance tests, ratings of training and experience, and oral interviews. All of these measures combine to form the best-known means of finding the right person for the right job.

II. HOW TO PASS THE WRITTEN TEST

A. *NATURE OF THE EXAMINATION*

To prepare intelligently for civil service examinations, you should know how they differ from school examinations you have taken. In school you were assigned certain definite pages to read or subjects to cover. The examination questions were quite detailed and usually emphasized memory. Civil service exams, on the other hand, try to discover your present ability to perform the duties of a position, plus your potentiality to learn these duties. In other words, a civil service exam attempts to predict how successful you will be. Questions cover such a broad area that they cannot be as minute and detailed as school exam questions.

In the public service similar kinds of work, or positions, are grouped together in one "class." This process is known as *position-classification*. All the positions in a class are paid according to the salary range for that class. One class title covers all of these positions, and they are all tested by the same examination.

B. *FOUR BASIC STEPS*

1) Study the announcement

How, then, can you know what subjects to study? Our best answer is: "Learn as much as possible about the class of positions for which you've applied." The exam will test the knowledge, skills and abilities needed to do the work.

Your most valuable source of information about the position you want is the official exam announcement. This announcement lists the training and experience qualifications. Check these standards and apply only if you come reasonably close to meeting them.

The brief description of the position in the examination announcement offers some clues to the subjects which will be tested. Think about the job itself. Review the duties in your mind. Can you perform them, or are there some in which you are rusty? Fill in the blank spots in your preparation.

Many jurisdictions preview the written test in the exam announcement by including a section called "Knowledge and Abilities Required," "Scope of the Examination," or some similar heading. Here you will find out specifically what fields will be tested.

2) Review your own background

Once you learn in general what the position is all about, and what you need to know to do the work, ask yourself which subjects you already know fairly well and which need improvement. You may wonder whether to concentrate on improving your strong areas or on building some background in your fields of weakness. When the announcement has specified "some knowledge" or "considerable knowledge," or has used adjectives like "beginning principles of…" or "advanced … methods," you can get a clue as to the number and difficulty of questions to be asked in any given field. More questions, and hence broader coverage, would be included for those subjects which are more important in the work. Now weigh your strengths and weaknesses against the job requirements and prepare accordingly.

3) Determine the level of the position

Another way to tell how intensively you should prepare is to understand the level of the job for which you are applying. Is it the entering level? In other words, is this the position in which beginners in a field of work are hired? Or is it an intermediate or advanced level? Sometimes this is indicated by such words as "Junior" or "Senior" in the class title. Other jurisdictions use Roman numerals to designate the level – Clerk I, Clerk II, for example. The word "Supervisor" sometimes appears in the title. If the level is not indicated by the title, check the description of duties. Will you be working under very close supervision, or will you have responsibility for independent decisions in this work?

4) Choose appropriate study materials

Now that you know the subjects to be examined and the relative amount of each subject to be covered, you can choose suitable study materials. For beginning level jobs, or even advanced ones, if you have a pronounced weakness in some aspect of your training, read a modern, standard textbook in that field. Be sure it is up to date and has general coverage. Such books are normally available at your library, and the librarian will be glad to help you locate one. For entry-level positions, questions of appropriate difficulty are chosen – neither highly advanced questions, nor those too simple. Such questions require careful thought but not advanced training.

If the position for which you are applying is technical or advanced, you will read more advanced, specialized material. If you are already familiar with the basic principles of your field, elementary textbooks would waste your time. Concentrate on advanced textbooks and technical periodicals. Think through the concepts and review difficult problems in your field.

These are all general sources. You can get more ideas on your own initiative, following these leads. For example, training manuals and publications of the government agency which employs workers in your field can be useful, particularly for technical and professional positions. A letter or visit to the government department involved may result in more specific study suggestions, and certainly will provide you with a more definite idea of the exact nature of the position you are seeking.

III. KINDS OF TESTS

Tests are used for purposes other than measuring knowledge and ability to perform specified duties. For some positions, it is equally important to test ability to make adjustments to new situations or to profit from training. In others, basic mental abilities not dependent on information are essential. Questions which test these things may not appear as pertinent to the duties of the position as those which test for knowledge and information. Yet they are often highly important parts of a fair examination. For very general questions, it is almost impossible to help you direct your study efforts. What we can do is to point out some of the more common of these general abilities needed in public service positions and describe some typical questions.

1) General information

Broad, general information has been found useful for predicting job success in some kinds of work. This is tested in a variety of ways, from vocabulary lists to questions about current events. Basic background in some field of work, such as sociology or economics, may be sampled in a group of questions. Often these are principles which have become familiar to most persons through exposure rather than through formal training. It is difficult to advise you how to study for these questions; being alert to the world around you is our best suggestion.

2) Verbal ability

An example of an ability needed in many positions is verbal or language ability. Verbal ability is, in brief, the ability to use and understand words. Vocabulary and grammar tests are typical measures of this ability. Reading comprehension or paragraph interpretation questions are common in many kinds of civil service tests. You are given a paragraph of written material and asked to find its central meaning.

3) Numerical ability
Number skills can be tested by the familiar arithmetic problem, by checking paired lists of numbers to see which are alike and which are different, or by interpreting charts and graphs. In the latter test, a graph may be printed in the test booklet which you are asked to use as the basis for answering questions.

4) Observation
A popular test for law-enforcement positions is the observation test. A picture is shown to you for several minutes, then taken away. Questions about the picture test your ability to observe both details and larger elements.

5) Following directions
In many positions in the public service, the employee must be able to carry out written instructions dependably and accurately. You may be given a chart with several columns, each column listing a variety of information. The questions require you to carry out directions involving the information given in the chart.

6) Skills and aptitudes
Performance tests effectively measure some manual skills and aptitudes. When the skill is one in which you are trained, such as typing or shorthand, you can practice. These tests are often very much like those given in business school or high school courses. For many of the other skills and aptitudes, however, no short-time preparation can be made. Skills and abilities natural to you or that you have developed throughout your lifetime are being tested.

Many of the general questions just described provide all the data needed to answer the questions and ask you to use your reasoning ability to find the answers. Your best preparation for these tests, as well as for tests of facts and ideas, is to be at your physical and mental best. You, no doubt, have your own methods of getting into an exam-taking mood and keeping "in shape." The next section lists some ideas on this subject.

IV. KINDS OF QUESTIONS

Only rarely is the "essay" question, which you answer in narrative form, used in civil service tests. Civil service tests are usually of the short-answer type. Full instructions for answering these questions will be given to you at the examination. But in case this is your first experience with short-answer questions and separate answer sheets, here is what you need to know:

1) Multiple-choice Questions
Most popular of the short-answer questions is the "multiple choice" or "best answer" question. It can be used, for example, to test for factual knowledge, ability to solve problems or judgment in meeting situations found at work.
A multiple-choice question is normally one of three types—
- It can begin with an incomplete statement followed by several possible endings. You are to find the one ending which *best* completes the statement, although some of the others may not be entirely wrong.
- It can also be a complete statement in the form of a question which is answered by choosing one of the statements listed.

- It can be in the form of a problem – again you select the best answer.

Here is an example of a multiple-choice question with a discussion which should give you some clues as to the method for choosing the right answer:

When an employee has a complaint about his assignment, the action which will *best* help him overcome his difficulty is to
- A. discuss his difficulty with his coworkers
- B. take the problem to the head of the organization
- C. take the problem to the person who gave him the assignment
- D. say nothing to anyone about his complaint

In answering this question, you should study each of the choices to find which is best. Consider choice "A" – Certainly an employee may discuss his complaint with fellow employees, but no change or improvement can result, and the complaint remains unresolved. Choice "B" is a poor choice since the head of the organization probably does not know what assignment you have been given, and taking your problem to him is known as "going over the head" of the supervisor. The supervisor, or person who made the assignment, is the person who can clarify it or correct any injustice. Choice "C" is, therefore, correct. To say nothing, as in choice "D," is unwise. Supervisors have and interest in knowing the problems employees are facing, and the employee is seeking a solution to his problem.

2) True/False Questions

The "true/false" or "right/wrong" form of question is sometimes used. Here a complete statement is given. Your job is to decide whether the statement is right or wrong.

SAMPLE: A roaming cell-phone call to a nearby city costs less than a non-roaming call to a distant city.

This statement is wrong, or false, since roaming calls are more expensive.

This is not a complete list of all possible question forms, although most of the others are variations of these common types. You will always get complete directions for answering questions. Be sure you understand *how* to mark your answers – ask questions until you do.

V. RECORDING YOUR ANSWERS

Computer terminals are used more and more today for many different kinds of exams.
For an examination with very few applicants, you may be told to record your answers in the test booklet itself. Separate answer sheets are much more common. If this separate answer sheet is to be scored by machine – and this is often the case – it is highly important that you mark your answers correctly in order to get credit.

An electronic scoring machine is often used in civil service offices because of the speed with which papers can be scored. Machine-scored answer sheets must be marked with a pencil, which will be given to you. This pencil has a high graphite content which responds to the electronic scoring machine. As a matter of fact, stray dots may register as answers, so do not let your pencil rest on the answer sheet while you are pondering the correct answer. Also, if your pencil lead breaks or is otherwise defective, ask for another.

Since the answer sheet will be dropped in a slot in the scoring machine, be careful not to bend the corners or get the paper crumpled.

The answer sheet normally has five vertical columns of numbers, with 30 numbers to a column. These numbers correspond to the question numbers in your test booklet. After each number, going across the page are four or five pairs of dotted lines. These short dotted lines have small letters or numbers above them. The first two pairs may also have a "T" or "F" above the letters. This indicates that the first two pairs only are to be used if the questions are of the true-false type. If the questions are multiple choice, disregard the "T" and "F" and pay attention only to the small letters or numbers.

Answer your questions in the manner of the sample that follows:

32. The largest city in the United States is
    A. Washington, D.C.
    B. New York City
    C. Chicago
    D. Detroit
    E. San Francisco

1) Choose the answer you think is best. (New York City is the largest, so "B" is correct.)
2) Find the row of dotted lines numbered the same as the question you are answering. (Find row number 32)
3) Find the pair of dotted lines corresponding to the answer. (Find the pair of lines under the mark "B.")
4) Make a solid black mark between the dotted lines.

VI. BEFORE THE TEST

Common sense will help you find procedures to follow to get ready for an examination. Too many of us, however, overlook these sensible measures. Indeed, nervousness and fatigue have been found to be the most serious reasons why applicants fail to do their best on civil service tests. Here is a list of reminders:

- Begin your preparation early – Don't wait until the last minute to go scurrying around for books and materials or to find out what the position is all about.
- Prepare continuously – An hour a night for a week is better than an all-night cram session. This has been definitely established. What is more, a night a week for a month will return better dividends than crowding your study into a shorter period of time.
- Locate the place of the exam – You have been sent a notice telling you when and where to report for the examination. If the location is in a different town or otherwise unfamiliar to you, it would be well to inquire the best route and learn something about the building.
- Relax the night before the test – Allow your mind to rest. Do not study at all that night. Plan some mild recreation or diversion; then go to bed early and get a good night's sleep.
- Get up early enough to make a leisurely trip to the place for the test – This way unforeseen events, traffic snarls, unfamiliar buildings, etc. will not upset you.
- Dress comfortably – A written test is not a fashion show. You will be known by number and not by name, so wear something comfortable.

- Leave excess paraphernalia at home – Shopping bags and odd bundles will get in your way. You need bring only the items mentioned in the official notice you received; usually everything you need is provided. Do not bring reference books to the exam. They will only confuse those last minutes and be taken away from you when in the test room.
- Arrive somewhat ahead of time – If because of transportation schedules you must get there very early, bring a newspaper or magazine to take your mind off yourself while waiting.
- Locate the examination room – When you have found the proper room, you will be directed to the seat or part of the room where you will sit. Sometimes you are given a sheet of instructions to read while you are waiting. Do not fill out any forms until you are told to do so; just read them and be prepared.
- Relax and prepare to listen to the instructions
- If you have any physical problem that may keep you from doing your best, be sure to tell the test administrator. If you are sick or in poor health, you really cannot do your best on the exam. You can come back and take the test some other time.

VII. AT THE TEST

The day of the test is here and you have the test booklet in your hand. The temptation to get going is very strong. Caution! There is more to success than knowing the right answers. You must know how to identify your papers and understand variations in the type of short-answer question used in this particular examination. Follow these suggestions for maximum results from your efforts:

1) Cooperate with the monitor

The test administrator has a duty to create a situation in which you can be as much at ease as possible. He will give instructions, tell you when to begin, check to see that you are marking your answer sheet correctly, and so on. He is not there to guard you, although he will see that your competitors do not take unfair advantage. He wants to help you do your best.

2) Listen to all instructions

Don't jump the gun! Wait until you understand all directions. In most civil service tests you get more time than you need to answer the questions. So don't be in a hurry. Read each word of instructions until you clearly understand the meaning. Study the examples, listen to all announcements and follow directions. Ask questions if you do not understand what to do.

3) Identify your papers

Civil service exams are usually identified by number only. You will be assigned a number; you must not put your name on your test papers. Be sure to copy your number correctly. Since more than one exam may be given, copy your exact examination title.

4) Plan your time

Unless you are told that a test is a "speed" or "rate of work" test, speed itself is usually not important. Time enough to answer all the questions will be provided, but this does not mean that you have all day. An overall time limit has been set. Divide the total time (in minutes) by the number of questions to determine the approximate time you have for each question.

5) Do not linger over difficult questions

If you come across a difficult question, mark it with a paper clip (useful to have along) and come back to it when you have been through the booklet. One caution if you do this – be sure to skip a number on your answer sheet as well. Check often to be sure that you have not lost your place and that you are marking in the row numbered the same as the question you are answering.

6) Read the questions

Be sure you know what the question asks! Many capable people are unsuccessful because they failed to *read* the questions correctly.

7) Answer all questions

Unless you have been instructed that a penalty will be deducted for incorrect answers, it is better to guess than to omit a question.

8) Speed tests

It is often better NOT to guess on speed tests. It has been found that on timed tests people are tempted to spend the last few seconds before time is called in marking answers at random – without even reading them – in the hope of picking up a few extra points. To discourage this practice, the instructions may warn you that your score will be "corrected" for guessing. That is, a penalty will be applied. The incorrect answers will be deducted from the correct ones, or some other penalty formula will be used.

9) Review your answers

If you finish before time is called, go back to the questions you guessed or omitted to give them further thought. Review other answers if you have time.

10) Return your test materials

If you are ready to leave before others have finished or time is called, take ALL your materials to the monitor and leave quietly. Never take any test material with you. The monitor can discover whose papers are not complete, and taking a test booklet may be grounds for disqualification.

VIII. EXAMINATION TECHNIQUES

1) Read the general instructions carefully. These are usually printed on the first page of the exam booklet. As a rule, these instructions refer to the timing of the examination; the fact that you should not start work until the signal and must stop work at a signal, etc. If there are any *special* instructions, such as a choice of questions to be answered, make sure that you note this instruction carefully.

2) When you are ready to start work on the examination, that is as soon as the signal has been given, read the instructions to each question booklet, underline any key words or phrases, such as *least, best, outline, describe* and the like. In this way you will tend to answer as requested rather than discover on reviewing your paper that you *listed without describing*, that you selected the *worst* choice rather than the *best* choice, etc.

3) If the examination is of the objective or multiple-choice type – that is, each question will also give a series of possible answers: A, B, C or D, and you are called upon to select the best answer and write the letter next to that answer on your answer paper – it is advisable to start answering each question in turn. There may be anywhere from 50 to 100 such questions in the three or four hours allotted and you can see how much time would be taken if you read through all the questions before beginning to answer any. Furthermore, if you come across a question or group of questions which you know would be difficult to answer, it would undoubtedly affect your handling of all the other questions.

4) If the examination is of the essay type and contains but a few questions, it is a moot point as to whether you should read all the questions before starting to answer any one. Of course, if you are given a choice – say five out of seven and the like – then it is essential to read all the questions so you can eliminate the two that are most difficult. If, however, you are asked to answer all the questions, there may be danger in trying to answer the easiest one first because you may find that you will spend too much time on it. The best technique is to answer the first question, then proceed to the second, etc.

5) Time your answers. Before the exam begins, write down the time it started, then add the time allowed for the examination and write down the time it must be completed, then divide the time available somewhat as follows:
    - If 3-1/2 hours are allowed, that would be 210 minutes. If you have 80 objective-type questions, that would be an average of 2-1/2 minutes per question. Allow yourself no more than 2 minutes per question, or a total of 160 minutes, which will permit about 50 minutes to review.
    - If for the time allotment of 210 minutes there are 7 essay questions to answer, that would average about 30 minutes a question. Give yourself only 25 minutes per question so that you have about 35 minutes to review.

6) The most important instruction is to *read each question* and make sure you know what is wanted. The second most important instruction is to *time yourself properly* so that you answer every question. The third most important instruction is to *answer every question*. Guess if you have to but include something for each question. Remember that you will receive no credit for a blank and will probably receive some credit if you write something in answer to an essay question. If you guess a letter – say "B" for a multiple-choice question – you may have guessed right. If you leave a blank as an answer to a multiple-choice question, the examiners may respect your feelings but it will not add a point to your score. Some exams may penalize you for wrong answers, so in such cases *only*, you may not want to guess unless you have some basis for your answer.

7) Suggestions
    a. Objective-type questions
        1. Examine the question booklet for proper sequence of pages and questions
        2. Read all instructions carefully
        3. Skip any question which seems too difficult; return to it after all other questions have been answered
        4. Apportion your time properly; do not spend too much time on any single question or group of questions

5. Note and underline key words – *all, most, fewest, least, best, worst, same, opposite,* etc.
6. Pay particular attention to negatives
7. Note unusual option, e.g., unduly long, short, complex, different or similar in content to the body of the question
8. Observe the use of "hedging" words – *probably, may, most likely,* etc.
9. Make sure that your answer is put next to the same number as the question
10. Do not second-guess unless you have good reason to believe the second answer is definitely more correct
11. Cross out original answer if you decide another answer is more accurate; do not erase until you are ready to hand your paper in
12. Answer all questions; guess unless instructed otherwise
13. Leave time for review

   b. Essay questions
   1. Read each question carefully
   2. Determine exactly what is wanted. Underline key words or phrases.
   3. Decide on outline or paragraph answer
   4. Include many different points and elements unless asked to develop any one or two points or elements
   5. Show impartiality by giving pros and cons unless directed to select one side only
   6. Make and write down any assumptions you find necessary to answer the questions
   7. Watch your English, grammar, punctuation and choice of words
   8. Time your answers; don't crowd material

8) Answering the essay question

Most essay questions can be answered by framing the specific response around several key words or ideas. Here are a few such key words or ideas:

M's: manpower, materials, methods, money, management
P's: purpose, program, policy, plan, procedure, practice, problems, pitfalls, personnel, public relations
   a. Six basic steps in handling problems:
   1. Preliminary plan and background development
   2. Collect information, data and facts
   3. Analyze and interpret information, data and facts
   4. Analyze and develop solutions as well as make recommendations
   5. Prepare report and sell recommendations
   6. Install recommendations and follow up effectiveness

   b. Pitfalls to avoid
   1. *Taking things for granted* – A statement of the situation does not necessarily imply that each of the elements is necessarily true; for example, a complaint may be invalid and biased so that all that can be taken for granted is that a complaint has been registered

2. *Considering only one side of a situation* – Wherever possible, indicate several alternatives and then point out the reasons you selected the best one
3. *Failing to indicate follow up* – Whenever your answer indicates action on your part, make certain that you will take proper follow-up action to see how successful your recommendations, procedures or actions turn out to be
4. *Taking too long in answering any single question* – Remember to time your answers properly

IX. AFTER THE TEST

Scoring procedures differ in detail among civil service jurisdictions although the general principles are the same. Whether the papers are hand-scored or graded by machine we have described, they are nearly always graded by number. That is, the person who marks the paper knows only the number – never the name – of the applicant. Not until all the papers have been graded will they be matched with names. If other tests, such as training and experience or oral interview ratings have been given, scores will be combined. Different parts of the examination usually have different weights. For example, the written test might count 60 percent of the final grade, and a rating of training and experience 40 percent. In many jurisdictions, veterans will have a certain number of points added to their grades.

After the final grade has been determined, the names are placed in grade order and an eligible list is established. There are various methods for resolving ties between those who get the same final grade – probably the most common is to place first the name of the person whose application was received first. Job offers are made from the eligible list in the order the names appear on it. You will be notified of your grade and your rank as soon as all these computations have been made. This will be done as rapidly as possible.

People who are found to meet the requirements in the announcement are called "eligibles." Their names are put on a list of eligible candidates. An eligible's chances of getting a job depend on how high he stands on this list and how fast agencies are filling jobs from the list.

When a job is to be filled from a list of eligibles, the agency asks for the names of people on the list of eligibles for that job. When the civil service commission receives this request, it sends to the agency the names of the three people highest on this list. Or, if the job to be filled has specialized requirements, the office sends the agency the names of the top three persons who meet these requirements from the general list.

The appointing officer makes a choice from among the three people whose names were sent to him. If the selected person accepts the appointment, the names of the others are put back on the list to be considered for future openings.

That is the rule in hiring from all kinds of eligible lists, whether they are for typist, carpenter, chemist, or something else. For every vacancy, the appointing officer has his choice of any one of the top three eligibles on the list. This explains why the person whose name is on top of the list sometimes does not get an appointment when some of the persons lower on the list do. If the appointing officer chooses the second or third eligible, the No. 1 eligible does not get a job at once, but stays on the list until he is appointed or the list is terminated.

X. HOW TO PASS THE INTERVIEW TEST

The examination for which you applied requires an oral interview test. You have already taken the written test and you are now being called for the interview test – the final part of the formal examination.

You may think that it is not possible to prepare for an interview test and that there are no procedures to follow during an interview. Our purpose is to point out some things you can do in advance that will help you and some good rules to follow and pitfalls to avoid while you are being interviewed.

What is an interview supposed to test?

The written examination is designed to test the technical knowledge and competence of the candidate; the oral is designed to evaluate intangible qualities, not readily measured otherwise, and to establish a list showing the relative fitness of each candidate – as measured against his competitors – for the position sought. Scoring is not on the basis of "right" and "wrong," but on a sliding scale of values ranging from "not passable" to "outstanding." As a matter of fact, it is possible to achieve a relatively low score without a single "incorrect" answer because of evident weakness in the qualities being measured.

Occasionally, an examination may consist entirely of an oral test – either an individual or a group oral. In such cases, information is sought concerning the technical knowledges and abilities of the candidate, since there has been no written examination for this purpose. More commonly, however, an oral test is used to supplement a written examination.

Who conducts interviews?

The composition of oral boards varies among different jurisdictions. In nearly all, a representative of the personnel department serves as chairman. One of the members of the board may be a representative of the department in which the candidate would work. In some cases, "outside experts" are used, and, frequently, a businessman or some other representative of the general public is asked to serve. Labor and management or other special groups may be represented. The aim is to secure the services of experts in the appropriate field.

However the board is composed, it is a good idea (and not at all improper or unethical) to ascertain in advance of the interview who the members are and what groups they represent. When you are introduced to them, you will have some idea of their backgrounds and interests, and at least you will not stutter and stammer over their names.

What should be done before the interview?

While knowledge about the board members is useful and takes some of the surprise element out of the interview, there is other preparation which is more substantive. It *is* possible to prepare for an oral interview – in several ways:

1) Keep a copy of your application and review it carefully before the interview

This may be the only document before the oral board, and the starting point of the interview. Know what education and experience you have listed there, and the sequence and dates of all of it. Sometimes the board will ask you to review the highlights of your experience for them; you should not have to hem and haw doing it.

2) Study the class specification and the examination announcement

Usually, the oral board has one or both of these to guide them. The qualities, characteristics or knowledges required by the position sought are stated in these documents. They offer valuable clues as to the nature of the oral interview. For example, if the job involves supervisory responsibilities, the announcement will usually indicate that knowledge of modern supervisory methods and the qualifications of the candidate as a supervisor will be tested. If so, you can expect such questions, frequently in the form of a hypothetical situation which you are expected to solve. NEVER go into an oral without knowledge of the duties and responsibilities of the job you seek.

3) Think through each qualification required

Try to visualize the kind of questions you would ask if you were a board member. How well could you answer them? Try especially to appraise your own knowledge and background in each area, *measured against the job sought*, and identify any areas in which you are weak. Be critical and realistic – do not flatter yourself.

4) Do some general reading in areas in which you feel you may be weak

For example, if the job involves supervision and your past experience has NOT, some general reading in supervisory methods and practices, particularly in the field of human relations, might be useful. Do NOT study agency procedures or detailed manuals. The oral board will be testing your understanding and capacity, not your memory.

5) Get a good night's sleep and watch your general health and mental attitude

You will want a clear head at the interview. Take care of a cold or any other minor ailment, and of course, no hangovers.

What should be done on the day of the interview?

Now comes the day of the interview itself. Give yourself plenty of time to get there. Plan to arrive somewhat ahead of the scheduled time, particularly if your appointment is in the fore part of the day. If a previous candidate fails to appear, the board might be ready for you a bit early. By early afternoon an oral board is almost invariably behind schedule if there are many candidates, and you may have to wait. Take along a book or magazine to read, or your application to review, but leave any extraneous material in the waiting room when you go in for your interview. In any event, relax and compose yourself.

The matter of dress is important. The board is forming impressions about you – from your experience, your manners, your attitude, and your appearance. Give your personal appearance careful attention. Dress your best, but not your flashiest. Choose conservative, appropriate clothing, and be sure it is immaculate. This is a business interview, and your appearance should indicate that you regard it as such. Besides, being well groomed and properly dressed will help boost your confidence.

Sooner or later, someone will call your name and escort you into the interview room. *This is it.* From here on you are on your own. It is too late for any more preparation. But remember, you asked for this opportunity to prove your fitness, and you are here because your request was granted.

What happens when you go in?

The usual sequence of events will be as follows: The clerk (who is often the board stenographer) will introduce you to the chairman of the oral board, who will introduce you to the other members of the board. Acknowledge the introductions before you sit down. Do not be surprised if you find a microphone facing you or a stenotypist sitting by. Oral interviews are usually recorded in the event of an appeal or other review.

Usually the chairman of the board will open the interview by reviewing the highlights of your education and work experience from your application – primarily for the benefit of the other members of the board, as well as to get the material into the record. Do not interrupt or comment unless there is an error or significant misinterpretation; if that is the case, do not hesitate. But do not quibble about insignificant matters. Also, he will usually ask you some question about your education, experience or your present job – partly to get you to start talking and to establish the interviewing "rapport." He may start the actual questioning, or turn it over to one of the other members. Frequently, each member undertakes the questioning on a particular area, one in which he is perhaps most competent, so you can expect each member to participate in the examination. Because time is limited, you may also expect some rather abrupt switches in the direction the questioning takes, so do not be upset by it. Normally, a board member will not pursue a single line of questioning unless he discovers a particular strength or weakness.

After each member has participated, the chairman will usually ask whether any member has any further questions, then will ask you if you have anything you wish to add. Unless you are expecting this question, it may floor you. Worse, it may start you off on an extended, extemporaneous speech. The board is not usually seeking more information. The question is principally to offer you a last opportunity to present further qualifications or to indicate that you have nothing to add. So, if you feel that a significant qualification or characteristic has been overlooked, it is proper to point it out in a sentence or so. Do not compliment the board on the thoroughness of their examination – they have been sketchy, and you know it. If you wish, merely say, "No thank you, I have nothing further to add." This is a point where you can "talk yourself out" of a good impression or fail to present an important bit of information. Remember, *you close the interview yourself*.

The chairman will then say, "That is all, Mr. _____, thank you." Do not be startled; the interview is over, and quicker than you think. Thank him, gather your belongings and take your leave. Save your sigh of relief for the other side of the door.

How to put your best foot forward

Throughout this entire process, you may feel that the board individually and collectively is trying to pierce your defenses, seek out your hidden weaknesses and embarrass and confuse you. Actually, this is not true. They are obliged to make an appraisal of your qualifications for the job you are seeking, and they want to see you in your best light. Remember, they must interview all candidates and a non-cooperative candidate may become a failure in spite of their best efforts to bring out his qualifications. Here are 15 suggestions that will help you:

1) Be natural – Keep your attitude confident, not cocky

If you are not confident that you can do the job, do not expect the board to be. Do not apologize for your weaknesses, try to bring out your strong points. The board is interested in a positive, not negative, presentation. Cockiness will antagonize any board member and make him wonder if you are covering up a weakness by a false show of strength.

2) Get comfortable, but don't lounge or sprawl

Sit erectly but not stiffly. A careless posture may lead the board to conclude that you are careless in other things, or at least that you are not impressed by the importance of the occasion. Either conclusion is natural, even if incorrect. Do not fuss with your clothing, a pencil or an ashtray. Your hands may occasionally be useful to emphasize a point; do not let them become a point of distraction.

3) Do not wisecrack or make small talk

This is a serious situation, and your attitude should show that you consider it as such. Further, the time of the board is limited – they do not want to waste it, and neither should you.

4) Do not exaggerate your experience or abilities

In the first place, from information in the application or other interviews and sources, the board may know more about you than you think. Secondly, you probably will not get away with it. An experienced board is rather adept at spotting such a situation, so do not take the chance.

5) If you know a board member, do not make a point of it, yet do not hide it

Certainly you are not fooling him, and probably not the other members of the board. Do not try to take advantage of your acquaintanceship – it will probably do you little good.

6) Do not dominate the interview

Let the board do that. They will give you the clues – do not assume that you have to do all the talking. Realize that the board has a number of questions to ask you, and do not try to take up all the interview time by showing off your extensive knowledge of the answer to the first one.

7) Be attentive

You only have 20 minutes or so, and you should keep your attention at its sharpest throughout. When a member is addressing a problem or question to you, give him your undivided attention. Address your reply principally to him, but do not exclude the other board members.

8) Do not interrupt

A board member may be stating a problem for you to analyze. He will ask you a question when the time comes. Let him state the problem, and wait for the question.

9) Make sure you understand the question

Do not try to answer until you are sure what the question is. If it is not clear, restate it in your own words or ask the board member to clarify it for you. However, do not haggle about minor elements.

10) Reply promptly but not hastily

A common entry on oral board rating sheets is "candidate responded readily," or "candidate hesitated in replies." Respond as promptly and quickly as you can, but do not jump to a hasty, ill-considered answer.

11) Do not be peremptory in your answers

A brief answer is proper – but do not fire your answer back. That is a losing game from your point of view. The board member can probably ask questions much faster than you can answer them.

12) Do not try to create the answer you think the board member wants

He is interested in what kind of mind you have and how it works – not in playing games. Furthermore, he can usually spot this practice and will actually grade you down on it.

13) Do not switch sides in your reply merely to agree with a board member

Frequently, a member will take a contrary position merely to draw you out and to see if you are willing and able to defend your point of view. Do not start a debate, yet do not surrender a good position. If a position is worth taking, it is worth defending.

14) Do not be afraid to admit an error in judgment if you are shown to be wrong

The board knows that you are forced to reply without any opportunity for careful consideration. Your answer may be demonstrably wrong. If so, admit it and get on with the interview.

15) Do not dwell at length on your present job

The opening question may relate to your present assignment. Answer the question but do not go into an extended discussion. You are being examined for a *new* job, not your present one. As a matter of fact, try to phrase ALL your answers in terms of the job for which you are being examined.

Basis of Rating

Probably you will forget most of these "do's" and "don'ts" when you walk into the oral interview room. Even remembering them all will not ensure you a passing grade. Perhaps you did not have the qualifications in the first place. But remembering them will help you to put your best foot forward, without treading on the toes of the board members.

Rumor and popular opinion to the contrary notwithstanding, an oral board wants you to make the best appearance possible. They know you are under pressure – but they also want to see how you respond to it as a guide to what your reaction would be under the pressures of the job you seek. They will be influenced by the degree of poise you display, the personal traits you show and the manner in which you respond.

ABOUT THIS BOOK

This book contains tests divided into Examination Sections. Go through each test, answering every question in the margin. We have also attached a sample answer sheet at the back of the book that can be removed and used. At the end of each test look at the answer key and check your answers. On the ones you got wrong, look at the right answer choice and learn. Do not fill in the answers first. Do not memorize the questions and answers, but understand the answer and principles involved. On your test, the questions will likely be different from the samples. Questions are changed and new ones added. If you understand these past questions you should have success with any changes that arise. Tests may consist of several types of questions. We have additional books on each subject should more study be advisable or necessary for you. Finally, the more you study, the better prepared you will be. This book is intended to be the last thing you study before you walk into the examination room. Prior study of relevant texts is also recommended. NLC publishes some of these in our Fundamental Series. Knowledge and good sense are important factors in passing your exam. Good luck also helps. So now study this Passbook, absorb the material contained within and take that knowledge into the examination. Then do your best to pass that exam.

EXAMINATION SECTION

EXAMINATION SECTION
TEST 1

DIRECTIONS: Each question or incomplete statement is followed by several suggested answers or completions. Select the one that BEST answers the question or completes the statement. *PRINT THE LETTER OF THE CORRECT ANSWER IN THE SPACE AT THE RIGHT.*

1. The one of the following which is the BEST reason for a medical social worker's having a sound foundation of medical information is that she may be able to

   A. determine the degree of disability which each illness may cause
   B. assist the doctors in bringing about solutions to medical problems
   C. instruct visiting nurses in case work
   D. instruct patients in the proper way to carry out medical recommendations
   E. work intelligently as a member of the medical team in helping sick people make the best use of medical care

   1.____

2. The one of the following which a medical social worker should consider the LEAST desirable during the course of the treatment interview with the client is to

   A. foster a totally dependent attitude
   B. respect the client's judgment
   C. permit the client to talk about possible solutions
   D. respect the client as an individual person
   E. clear the air and let the client talk

   2.____

3. The one of the following which is MOST likely to be the medical social worker's role with a clinic patient who has a mild case of diabetes is to

   A. help the patient change his environment
   B. help the patient accept his illness
   C. arrange for the placement of his children
   D. arrange for blood sugar tests
   E. arrange convalescent care

   3.____

4. The one of the following which is the PRIMARY purpose of the teaching of medical students by a medical social worker is to

   A. impress upon them the responsibilities of the medical social worker
   B. increase the number of referrals to the medical social worker
   C. make them aware of the social and emotional factors which may complicate the care of patients
   D. describe the development of social work to them
   E. teach them medical social casework

   4.____

5. The one of the following functions which is agreed by medical social work authorities to be the PROPER focus of a modern medical social service department is

   A. teaching social aspects of medicine
   B. assisting in research
   C. providing medical relief
   D. completing brief service cases
   E. performing casework

   5.____

1

6. Medical social work authorities consider a 100% review of a diagnostic group in a hospital an appropriate activity of a medical social worker under certain circumstances PROVIDED the purpose is

    A. individualization
    B. health education
    C. transference
    D. steering
    E. medical follow-up

7. In addition to basic knowledge of social work, the one of the following in which medical social workers are expected to have SPECIAL ability is

    A. recognizing the symptoms of early illness
    B. first aid
    C. follow-up of tuberculosis contacts
    D. working in a team-work relationship with other professions in a medical agency
    E. planning recreation programs in hospital wards

8. The administrator of a hospital is responsible for the total functioning of the institution, and each department head is responsible to the administrator for the proper functioning of his department. Assuming that you are a medical social worker in the hospital and a student nurse is extremely insolent to you or to a patient in your presence, the one of the following to whom you should report her action is

    A. the doctor on service
    B. the director of nurses
    C. your immediate supervisor
    D. the registered nurse on the floor
    E. the hospital administrator

9. An acutely ill mother of a healthy two-week old infant girl is admitted to a hospital at night. The following morning, the husband of the patient phones the medical social worker on the service and demands to know why the baby was refused readmission to the hospital nursery when it only left there the week before.
    The one of the following replies which the medical social worker SHOULD give to the husband is that

    A. there are no vacant bassinets in the nursery
    B. the baby was not admitted to the nursery because she is not sick
    C. if social service had been on duty, the baby would have been admitted
    D. he should report the matter to the medical superintendent
    E. infants are never admitted to the nursery from outside the hospital

10. The one of the following which is the PRIMARY role of social casework is to

    A. direct people who have little knowledge of life toward more satisfying experiences
    B. readjust environmental factors which are hindering a person's social adjustment
    C. help people recognize and handle problems which are not beyond their capacity to solve
    D. give sympathetic understanding to individuals who have social problems
    E. refer individuals to the proper community resource to meet their needs

11. The one of the following which is the PRIME requisite of a good social worker is a

    A. respect for the worth of an individual
    B. high degree of intelligence
    C. knowledge of psychiatry and mental hygiene
    D. sound knowledge of resources
    E. good knowledge of human behavior

12. Of the following, the one which is the BEST definition of social casework is

    A. a substitute for proper family relations
    B. a treatment process for sick persons
    C. a method of mass treatment of social problems
    D. an individual approach to people in trouble
    E. a method of solving financial problems

13. The one of the following which may be said to have come FIRST in the history and development of social work as a profession is

    A. analytical assistance
    B. friendly visiting by volunteer workers
    C. psychological approach
    D. outdoor relief
    E. social diagnoses

14. The one of the following circumstances in which casework service would be MOST likely to bring about a *successful* solution is in a situation in which

    A. a family is satisfied with things as they are
    B. the attitudes and habits of a patient are firmly entrenched and of long standing
    C. for one reason or another, there is only financial need
    D. the worker is working for the community against the desires of the patient
    E. a family seeks help with the problem of an adolescent child

15. The one of the following which is an IDEAL social casework situation is a(n)

    A. prisoner released from a reformatory who is very penitent for his crime
    B. person who is pronounced cured of congenital syphilis
    C. unwed mother who is seeking assistance by court action to punish the putative father
    D. psychoneurotic patient who is aware that her problems come from within her environment and her reaction to this environment
    E. person who knows he needs help, is capable of cooperating, and seeks some solution to his problem

16. In distinguishing between functions of a public agency and a private agency, the one of the following functions which would MOST likely belong only to a private agency is to

    A. investigate occupational resources
    B. investigate need for complete financial assistance
    C. evaluate need of an individual for rehabilitation
    D. do casework with the marginal income group
    E. determine budgetary needs of the indigent group

17. The one of the following services to patients which is not considered as legitimately falling within the functions of the medical social service department of a hospital is the

    A. securing of appliances
    B. arranging for convalescent care
    C. arranging for day care for children
    D. dispensing of medications
    E. reporting to community agencies

17._____

18. A voluntary hospital is a hospital

    A. in which doctors are forbidden to accept fees
    B. which accepts only patients unable to pay the full cost of their care
    C. which is entirely supported by public contributions
    D. in which most of the hospital workers are volunteers
    E. which is a non-profit institution

18._____

19. The one of the following which is a TRUE statement regarding the commissioner of hospitals is that he is

    A. responsible for the health of all residents of the city
    B. appointed by the mayor
    C. required to sign all commitment papers
    D. responsible only to the governor of the state
    E. an elected official for a two-year term

19._____

20. The one of the following which is a TRUE statement is that medical care in a tax-supported hospital is available to

    A. only those who have settlement in the area
    B. only those receiving public assistance
    C. all persons in need of medical treatment
    D. emergency cases only
    E. persons with contagious diseases only

20._____

21. The one of the following which is the PRIMARY function of the department of health is

    A. the treatment of contagious diseases
    B. education of the public towards better health
    C. conducting statistical research in problems of health
    D. providing nursing service to the indigent
    E. the distribution of health literature

21._____

22. A premarital blood test is required prior to the issuance of a marriage license. This requirement may be waived when

    A. both parties have been married before to different spouses
    B. the woman is pregnant at the time the marriage license is requested
    C. both parties have had physical examinations by a private physician
    D. both parties present reports of negative blood tests taken 6 months prior to the request for a license
    E. the man is over 65 years of age and in apparent good health

22._____

23. The one of the following statements regarding the care and treatment of tuberculous patients in the state which is FALSE is:

    A. If it is established that an alien was suffering from tuberculosis at the time of landing or becomes a public charge as a result of this condition within five years, he is eligible for sanitarium care for a one-year period in a federal hospital
    B. Any person affected with a communicable disease such as tuberculosis, likely to be dangerous to the lives and health of other persons, may be removed to a hospital designated by a board of health, upon the report of a duly authorized physician
    C. Care and treatment provided by the state or by any county or city for persons suffering from tuberculosis shall be available without cost or charge to any person having state residence and at the discretion of the state commissioner of health to any other person in the state who is suffering from tuberculosis
    D. Persons approved for admission to state hospitals unable to pay for transportation may be furnished such transportation by the superintendent of the hospital, and that transportation to another hospital for special care and treatment may also be furnished
    E. Any person who volunteers to assume and pay for the cost of the care and treatment of a patient suffering from tuberculosis shall be permitted to do so, but no state, county, city, or other public official shall request or require such payment

24. The one of the following which forms a PRIMARY aim of school child guidance clinics is the

    A. treatment of the parents
    B. prevention of juvenile delinquency
    C. prevention of mental ill health
    D. prevention of truancy
    E. treatment of the narcotic addict

25. The Community Chest and the Council of Social Agencies in cities where both exist work cooperatively to provide the greatest welfare for the entire community. The one of the following functions which would fall EXCLUSIVELY within the functions of the Community Chest is to

    A. give group work service to the community
    B. provide recreational facilities to members
    C. support agency functions and programs
    D. raise funds for the social welfare and health agencies
    E. interpret the work of individual agencies

26. The one of the following which is the PRIMARY function of the Tuberculosis and Health Association is

    A. psychometric testing   B. convalescent care
    C. education of the public   D. financial assistance
    E. surgical treatment

27. The one of the following which is the CHIEF purpose of the visits paid by a public health nurse to a patient in his home is to

    A. educate patient or patient group to give adequate care
    B. make epidemiological investigations
    C. report to the truant authority
    D. give reassurance to patient and patient group
    E. evaluate the home situation for emotional and physical strains

28. When a post-partum patient and her baby are discharged after a week in a hospital and the case is referred to the Visiting Nurse Service, the one of the following which is the USUAL routine for the visiting nurse is to

    A. visit daily for the next week to check on the mother's condition and to bathe the baby
    B. arrange for housekeeping service if it seems necessary
    C. keep in touch with the nurse in the school attended by other children in the family to avoid exposing the baby to a communicable disease
    D. keep the referral on file unless the patient is under a physician's care at home
    E. visit within a short time of the patient's return home to instruct her in the care of the baby

29. A 35-year-old woman who had always lived in New York City was diagnosed as having osteomyelitis of the left tibia, and was admitted to a New York City hospital for treatment. Conservative treatment was of no avail, and she had an amputation below the left knee. The medical social worker was called in to see her as she said she had spent five months in San Francisco, California, just prior to her hospitalization and had no means of support. She needed an artificial leg before leaving the hospital, plus financial support. Before her illness, she was a typist.
    The one of the following agencies which should be contacted FIRST is the

    A. New York State Department of Social Services
    B. California State Department of Welfare
    C. New York State Division of Vocational Rehabilitation
    D. Welfare Council of New York City
    E. Rehabilitation Division of the New York City Department of Hospitals

30. When the woman described in the preceding question was ready to leave the hospital and the medical social worker was seeking financial support for maintenance, the one of the following agencies which SHOULD be contacted is the

    A. Department of Social Services
    B. Florence Crittenton League
    C. Division of Placement and Unemployment Insurance
    D. Workmen's Compensation Office
    E. Community Service Society

31. The name of the following institutions which is NOT under the management and control of the State Department of Correction is the 31.____

   A. Berkshire Industrial Farm
   B. Wallkill Prison
   C. Woodbourne Correctional Institution
   D. Elmira Reformatory
   E. State Vocational Institution

32. The one of the following which can be considered the PRIMARY purpose of the Social Security Act is the 32.____

   A. insurance against loss of earnings by an injured employee
   B. furthering of the security of the citizen and his family through social insurance
   C. distribution of surplus wealth among the needy classes
   D. development of an economic balance between the wealthy and the poor
   E. insurance of dependents against need

33. The passage of the Social Security Act in 1935 points toward the establishment of a broad national welfare program. The one of the following ways in which federal funds are provided, according to the provisions of the Act, is through 33.____

   A. payment of all the administrative funds used in disbursing state and local funds
   B. maintenance of adequate institutions to foster a good national program
   C. lump sum payments to all needy blind and widows
   D. part payment in participation with state and local funds
   E. full payment to individual recipients

34. The one of the following groups of persons which is ELIGIBLE for benefits under the Social Security Act is 34.____

   A. persons who have worked a required period of time in certain covered occupations
   B. the dependents of workmen injured or killed while on the job
   C. all those over 65 years old who are unable to find employment
   D. the dependents of soldiers, sailors, or marines killed while on combat duty
   E. all citizens who have reached the age of 65 years, whether or not in need of financial assistance

35. Of the following categories, the one which was MOST recently added to those which are covered under the Social Security Act is 35.____

   A. the blind
   B. the permanently disabled
   C. crippled adults
   D. the aged
   E. dependent children

KEY (CORRECT ANSWERS)

1. E	11. A	21. B	31. A
2. A	12. D	22. B	32. B
3. B	13. B	23. A	33. D
4. C	14. E	24. C	34. A
5. E	15. E	25. D	35. B
6. A	16. D	26. C	
7. D	17. D	27. A	
8. C	18. E	28. E	
9. E	19. B	29. C	
10. C	20. C	30. A	

EXAMINATION SECTION
TEST 1

DIRECTIONS: Each question or incomplete statement is followed by several suggested answers or completions. Select the one that BEST answers the question or completes the statement. *PRINT THE LETTER OF THE CORRECT ANSWER IN THE SPACE AT THE RIGHT.*

1. Social case work is PRIMARILY

    A. a method of preventing juvenile delinquency
    B. the art of listening to others
    C. an interpretation to lay persons of social problems
    D. the determination of the individual's ability to meet situations
    E. an individual approach to people in trouble

    1._____

2. Statistics show that the MAJORITY of people *initially* go to social agencies for

    A. recreational purposes
    B. help with financial problems
    C. vocational guidance
    D. help with marital problems
    E. help with emotional problems

    2._____

3. Of the following, the trend followed by public welfare agencies at the present time is to

    A. give *relief in kind* to avoid wasteful spending of money
    B. give food and clothing vouchers on short-term cases
    C. discourage work relief projects
    D. give *cash relief* where the financial need has been established
    E. make public lists of relief recipients

    3._____

4. In the initial interview with a client, the one of the following which is the MOST important is for the medical social worker to

    A. establish a sound social diagnosis
    B. outline the functions of her agency
    C. be aware of treatment possibilities
    D. listen closely and plan treatment
    E. determine what the client sees as the problem

    4._____

5. The one of the following which is the PRIMARY function of a medical social consultant in a family welfare agency is to

    A. carry a case load of families having medical problems
    B. interpret the medical diagnoses to the clients
    C. confer directly with doctors concerning the clients' medical needs
    D. study the health needs of the families
    E. assist the case workers in the handling of medical problems

    5._____

6. The one of the following which is the PRIMARY function of the family welfare agency is to

   A. provide convalescent care for sick children
   B. establish need and eligibility for proper housing for low income families in order to meet minimum health standards
   C. supervise family relations, thereby insuring the welfare and prevention of delinquency of children
   D. offer vocational rehabilitation services and encourage employment of the handicapped person
   E. help individuals and families meet problems and make the best possible adjustment within their limitations

7. The one of the following social workers who is well-known for her work in social diagnosis is

   A. Bertha Reynolds
   B. Janet Thornton
   C. Antoinette Cannon
   D. Harriet Bartlett
   E. Mabel McGuire

8. The one of the following which is the PRIMARY function of the social service exchange is to

   A. distinguish the frauds from the needy cases in almsgiving
   B. promote more efficient service to individuals
   C. discourage professional begging through the recording system
   D. insure a fair distribution of welfare funds to agencies
   E. distinguish worthy from unworthy families prior to giving assistance

9. The one of the following which is NOT considered a function of the private family agency is the

   A. rehabilitation of the handicapped through *sheltered employment*
   B. planning of summer camp placements for underprivileged children
   C. assisting of unwed mothers in planning for adoption of their babies
   D. giving of consultant and referral service for the indigent
   E. giving of supplemental financial assistance to marginal income families

10. The author of SOCIAL WORK RECORDING is

    A. Grace White
    B. Bertha Reynolds
    C. Gordon Hamilton
    D. Richard Cabot
    E. Carol Cooley

11. The one of the following functions which should NEVER be assumed by a medical social worker in a hospital is

    A. planning convalescent care for private patients
    B. routine social review for certain groups
    C. accepting surrenders of babies for adoption
    D. social admitting of indigent patients
    E. terminal care planning, if necessary

12. The one of the following which is the PRIMARY responsibility of any hospital is to   12._____
    A. keep adequate records on all patients
    B. train the medical staff adequately
    C. assist in the advancement of medical knowledge
    D. render care to the sick and injured
    E. promote community health and wellbeing

13. As the medical social worker in a hospital, you have submitted the necessary forms to   13._____
    the Department of Social Services for a prenatal patient to be granted elastic stockings
    because of severe varicosities. After four weeks have elapsed, the patient reports that
    she has not received the stockings.
    The one of the following procedures which you should follow is to

    A. call the social investigator on the case
    B. notify the investigato's supervisor
    C. tell the patient that such matters take a long time
    D. purchase stockings through hospital funds
    E. call the appropriate medical social worker at the Department of Social Services

14. The one of the following which is the PRIMARY function of the social case work supervi-   14._____
    sor in a hospital setting is to

    A. act as a liaison between the administration and the workers
    B. assist and teach her workers to do their job adequately
    C. teach workers, doctors, and nurses the value of case work
    D. administer the expenditures of funds
    E. determine policies of the department as they affect the hospital

15. Assume that as the medical social worker in a hospital, you are called to the accident   15._____
    ward. The doctor states that the unconscious woman on the table has had a miscarriage
    and it will be necessary to admit her for a curettage. Her four children, age 6, 4, 3, and 2,
    are in the waiting room of the hospital. Police report that there are no relatives at the
    address given.
    The one of the following which should be your FIRST step in the case is to

    A. clear the case with social service exchange
    B. call the child care division of the Department of Social Services
    C. arrange for homemaker service
    D. place the children in an emergency shelter
    E. take the children to the Speedwell Society

16. A patient in a voluntary hospital dispensary is in need of a regular supply of bandages and sterile dressings because of a diagnosis of incurable cancer. The patient's family who has been supporting him is unable to meet this additional expense.
The one of the following which would be the BEST procedure for the medical social worker in the hospital to follow is to

   A. send the patient to a city hospital which by law must provide dressings
   B. obtain the necessary form from the Department of Social Services to authorize the hospital pharmacy to dispense these articles
   C. advise the patient to make bandages and sterile dressings
   D. send an order in duplicate for these to the Department of Social Services
   E. contact the local chapter of the American Cancer Society

16.____

17. Suppose that a patient in a voluntary hospital is to be transferred to a nursing home in another borough of the city. She has no funds to pay for transportation by an ambulance.
Of the following, transfer by ambulance should be arranged through the

   A. Department of Hospitals
   B. Social Service Department of a private hospital
   C. Department of Health
   D. Department of Social Services
   E. Shut-In Society

17.____

18. The one of the following statements which is TRUE in regard to the voluntary, non-profit hospitals is that

   A. they are exempt from paying taxes
   B. patients must subject themselves for research purposes
   C. payments may be made only for the exact cost of medical care
   D. the Department of Health has no control over them
   E. no doctor may receive compensation for services rendered

18.____

19. Of the following, the CHIEF value of the medical social worker's attendance at ward rounds and conferences with the doctors on service is that

   A. knowledge of medical matters gives security to the worker
   B. the social and medical planning can be coordinated
   C. the worker can report verbally to the doctor rather than dictate extensive records
   D. the patient sees the worker as a part of the medical team
   E. the doctors find it convenient to make referrals at that time

19.____

20. The one of the following to whom the director of the social service department of a voluntary hospital is generally responsible is the

   A. United Hospital Fund
   B. board of managers
   C. director of nurses
   D. hospital administrator
   E. medical advisory committee

20.____

21. Volunteers can be an asset in the functioning of any hospital. 21.____
The one of the following which represents their GREATEST value to the hospital from the point of view of public relations is

   A. interpreting the hospital to the community
   B. popularizing the hospital with the patients by meeting their personal needs
   C. replacing employees during the labor shortage
   D. lowering the cost of caring for the sick
   E. giving service to visiting relatives which might not otherwise be available

22. The one of the following hospitals which is operated by the Department of Hospitals is 22.____

   A. the Hospital for Joint Diseases
   B. Columbus Hospital
   C. Gouverneur Hospital
   D. Brooklyn Thoracic Hospital
   E. Montefiore Hospital

23. Assume that you are the medical social worker in a clinic. A patient complains to you 23.____
about the time involved in clinic attendance, questioning particularly the need for repeated clinic visits prior to his being given treatment recommendations.
The one of the following you should do FIRST is to

   A. explain that the doctors give their time free, and patience is necessary
   B. interpret the needs of each patient who is waiting at the clinic at the time
   C. describe the overcrowding and the need for better community resources
   D. interpret the possible necessity of laboratory procedures prior to accurate diagnosis and treatment measures
   E. discuss the length of time involved in visiting a private doctor during his office hours

24. If a forty-year-old woman with severe rheumatic heart disease requests her doctor to 24.____
sterilize her by a tubal ligation, he may do so legally PROVIDED he

   A. can testify that further pregnancies would be dangerous
   B. has the consent of the woman with two witnesses present
   C. has the signed consent of the woman and her husband
   D. explains the nature of the operation to the woman and her husband
   E. has a court order to perform the operation

25. In regard to the care of the chronically ill, the one of the following which is recommended 25.____
CHIEFLY is the

   A. establishment of more chronic hospitals specifically designated as caring only for the chronically ill
   B. establishment of more hospital facilities for their care in the community general hospitals
   C. placing of greater responsibility for their care upon relatives and friends
   D. payment of larger fees to the privately owned nursing homes
   E. conduct of research into the causes of chronic illness by a greater number of voluntary hospitals

KEY (CORRECT ANSWERS)

1. E
2. B
3. D
4. E
5. E

6. E
7. A
8. B
9. E
10. C

11. C
12. D
13. E
14. B
15. B

16. E
17. A
18. A
19. B
20. D

21. A
22. C
23. D
24. C
25. B

TEST 2

DIRECTIONS: Each question or incomplete statement is followed by several suggested answers or completions. Select the one that BEST answers the question or completes the statement. *PRINT THE LETTER OF THE CORRECT ANSWER IN THE SPACE AT THE RIGHT.*

1. It is important for a medical social worker to have a basic knowledge of medical information MAINLY because

    A. in working with the doctor she must prove her competence
    B. patients will ask pertinent questions regarding diagnosis and treatment of their illnesses
    C. she can encourage patients to maintain good health standards
    D. the social problems of the patients may vary according to the nature of their illnesses
    E. she can help patients to avoid the major illnesses

2. In order to be admitted to a state tuberculosis sanitarium, the patient MUST

    A. be diagnosed as an active tuberculosis case
    B. be unable to pay for private care
    C. have legal residence in the state
    D. apply for admission through the division of handicapped
    E. commit himself

3. The one of the following which is the PRIMARY aim of public health programs in relation to illness and disease is to

    A. cure
    B. palliate
    C. prevent
    D. conduct research
    E. ameliorate

4. Every child before admission to school is required to be vaccinated against

    A. smallpox
    B. diphtheria
    C. typhoid
    D. scarlet fever
    E. whooping cough

5. Cancer is considered a public health responsibility MAINLY because of the

    A. enormity of the problem
    B. lack of adequate diagnostic facilities
    C. need for research
    D. familial disposition
    E. value of contact examination

6. The one of the following whom the U.S. Children's Bureau would NOT consider a crippled or a handicapped child is a child with

    A. cerebral palsy
    B. nephrosis
    C. poliomyelitis
    D. a cardiac disorder
    E. a club foot

7. The one of the following which is the PRIMARY function of the American Heart Association is

   A. fundraising for indigent patients
   B. promotion of research
   C. provision of convalescent facilities
   D. education of the public
   E. supervision of heart clinics

8. The one of the following which is NOT a function of the visiting nurse organizations is

   A. relief of the sick in their homes
   B. giving injections to patients at home
   C. supervising health care of the newborn at home
   D. education of the patient group to give adequate care to the patient
   E. full-time bedside nursing care in the home

9. The father of a man in the armed forces became seriously ill and was hospitalized in a critical condition. He kept calling for his son, who was stationed in this country. The one of the following you would call in order to ask that the son be granted a leave to see his father is the

   A. American Legion
   B. son's commanding officer
   C. Veterans Administration
   D. Traveler's Aid Society
   E. American Red Cross

10. The one of the following which is a convalescent home for the care of cardiac patients with rheumatic fever is

    A. Elizabeth House
    B. Eleanora's Home
    C. Francis Sanatorium
    D. Charles Hospital
    E. Giles' Home

11. The one of the following which BEST describes the Welfare Council is:

    A. A council of agencies to decide upon the functioning of each member agency
    B. A group of lay persons whose function is to insure good welfare practices
    C. A council of wealthy citizens, with one paid employee, to give informational service
    D. A council of social agencies to coordinate existing welfare services
    E. The central channel for the collection and distribution of welfare funds

12. The one of the following agencies which is NOT a settlement house is the

    A. Hudson Guild
    B. House of St. Giles
    C. Casita Maria
    D. Greenwich House
    E. Hartley House

13. The one of the following circumstances which will warrant a 'home teacher' for a child registered in a grammar school is if

    A. he is registered in a public school
    B. he will be unable to attend regular school for at least a month
    C. he has been known to suffer from a lack of schooling
    D. his family is agreeable to the plan and will cooperate
    E. his intelligence quotient demonstrates he will benefit by this

14. In order to have a child admitted to the Willowbrook Hospital, application must be made to the

    A. City Department of Hospitals
    B. City Department of Health
    C. State Department of Mental Hygiene
    D. State Board of Social Services
    E. City Department of Correction

15. There are no private or voluntary hospitals in the city whose PRIMARY function is the treatment of

    A. orthopedic diseases
    B. the chronically ill
    C. cancer
    D. nervous diseases
    E. contagious diseases

16. Of the following, those who are legally entitled to special preference when applying for housing through the Housing Authority are

    A. handicapped persons
    B. persons in the lowest income group
    C. persons in rooming houses
    D. honorably discharged veterans
    E. families with many children

17. The one of the following which is the PRIMARY purpose of the Worker's Compensation Law is to

    A. protect both the employer and the employee
    B. insure full pay to sick workers
    C. insure favorable work conditions in dangerous positions
    D. eliminate *sweat shop labor* and maintain adequate wages
    E. replace the need for unions in large factories

18. A person whose employment comes within the provisions of the State Unemployment Compensation Act, upon losing his position, is ALWAYS entitled to receive unemployment compensation if he

    A. is unable to obtain work in his specialized field
    B. applies for compensation within 48 hours of the termination of his employment
    C. has worked in certain occupations for a specific number of quarters in the previous year
    D. is able to prove that he lost his employment through no fault of his own
    E. can prove that his family will be in need until he obtains employment again

19. A legally married woman who has been living continuously with her husband bears a child who she claims is not her husband's child.
    The one of the following statements which is TRUE in connection with the placing of this child for legal adoption is that the

    A. alleged father must give his consent for adoption
    B. mother alone is required to give her consent for adoption
    C. child cannot be adopted legally
    D. alleged father must prove the child was his
    E. woman's husband must give his consent for adoption

19.____

20. Many states have passed the so-called disability benefit laws.
    The one of the following which is a TRUE statement in connection with these laws is that

    A. cash benefits for occupational injuries or illnesses are paid
    B. the employer must pay all employees half salary when illness occurs
    C. both employees and employers are covered by insurance to meet the cost of their illness
    D. cash benefits are paid to workers who lose wages because of non-occupational illness or accident
    E. the federal government will pay administrative costs of enforcement

20.____

KEY (CORRECT ANSWERS)

1.	D	11.	D
2.	A	12.	B
3.	C	13.	B
4.	A	14.	C
5.	A	15.	E
6.	B	16.	D
7.	D	17.	A
8.	E	18.	C
9.	E	19.	E
10.	C	20.	D

TEST 3

DIRECTIONS: Each question or incomplete statement is followed by several suggested answers or completions. Select the one that BEST answers the question or completes the statement. *PRINT THE LETTER OF THE CORRECT ANSWER IN THE SPACE AT THE RIGHT.*

1. The one of the following which is a TRUE statement about the Social Security Act is that it   1.____

    A. provides with a pension everyone who is over 65 years old
    B. ensures financial security for children of aged parents
    C. provides a minimum economic basic security for millions
    D. eliminates poverty under our present economy
    E. provides employment for the older age group

2. The one of the following which was MOST recently added to the categories of federal public assistance is   2.____

    A. aid to the permanently disabled
    B. aid to dependent children
    C. aid to the blind
    D. old age assistance
    E. home relief

3. Of the following statements relating to social security, the one which is TRUE is that   3.____

    A. a person receiving a monthly social security check may receive supplementary assistance from the Department of Social Services
    B. every person over 65 years of age is entitled to benefits through the Bureau of Old Age and Survivors' Insurance
    C. a person must give positive proof that he is in need and has no relatives to assist him before he is eligible for a social security check
    D. a person who lives in an old age home is not eligible to receive a social security check
    E. a person may receive a social security check while he is working provided he does not earn over $5,000 a year

4. Under the social security laws, a mother with children under 16 years may ALWAYS obtain an Aid to Dependent Children allotment if   4.____

    A. her husband is killed in the line of duty in the United States Armed Services
    B. she proves that, due to her husband's illness or death, the family is in financial need
    C. she is widowed and is unable to obtain gainful employment
    D. she has demonstrated that it is necessary for her to remain at home with her children
    E. the husband has deserted the family

5. The one of the following programs which is administered and operated ONLY by the federal government is

   A. services for crippled children
   B. aid to the needy blind
   C. aid to dependent children
   D. old age and survivors' insurance
   E. aid to the permanently disabled

6. Under the Department of Health, Education, and Welfare, there is provision for a federal-state program of vocational rehabilitation.
   The one of the following which is the BASIC objective of the total program is to

   A. prevent disabling diseases
   B. restore disabled persons in body and spirit
   C. provide appliances where necessary
   D. rehabilitate the mentally defective
   E. retrain disabled servicemen

7. The one of the following agencies which administers the U.S. Public Health Service is the

   A. U.S. Children's Bureau
   B. Treasury Department
   C. National Security Resources Board
   D. National Research Council
   E. Department of Health, Education and Welfare

8. The one of the following which historically was the FIRST function of what is now the U.S. Public Health Service is

   A. the provision of medical and hospital care for the nation's merchant seamen
   B. research into the causes of contagious diseases
   C. the establishment of the Pure Food and Drug Act
   D. the provision of care for the mentally disturbed
   E. administration of city and state departments of health

9. The one of the following U.S. Public Health Service hospitals which gives treatment to narcotic addicts is the

   A. Freedmen's Hospital, Washington, D.C.
   B. Carville Hospital, Carville, La.
   C. U.S. Public Health Service Hospital, Lexington, Ky.
   D. U.S. Public Health Service Hospital, Stapleton, S.I., N.Y.
   E. U.S. Public Health Service Hospital, Manhattan Beach, Brooklyn, N.Y.

Questions 10-15.

DIRECTIONS: Questions 10 through 15 are to be answered SOLELY on the basis of the facts given below.

CASE A

A forty-eight-year old single woman who has Parkinson's syndrome comes to the dispensary of a voluntary general hospital for treatment of excessive vaginal bleeding. She is admitted to the hospital as a *City case* after she proves that she is supported by a Department of Social Services allowance. She has been living in a furnished room and has been receiving a restaurant allowance. A biopsy is done, and a diagnosis of advanced carcinoma of the cervix is made. The hospital is not equipped to treat the patient and wishes her transferred to a city hospital for surgery.

10. As a *City case,* the one of the following statements which is TRUE is that

    A. only emergency treatment pending transfer to the city hospital will be rendered
    B. the city will assume the complete cost of any medical care rendered
    C. the patient's welfare checks will be used to pay her hospital expenses
    D. the voluntary hospital will be reimbursed by the city for care given on a per diem basis
    E. as a non-paying patient, she agrees to enter the voluntary hospital for diagnostic and research purposes only

11. Of the following, the BEST definition of biopsy is

    A. an examination of the substance obtained through a gastric lavage
    B. the removal and microscopic examination of a piece of tissue
    C. a laboratory examination of vaginal bleeding
    D. a blood test showing cancer cells in the bloodstream
    E. a fluoroscopic examination of a body organ

12. The one of the following departments which may authorize the transfer of this patient from the voluntary to the city hospital is the

    A. Department of Social Services
    B. Police Department
    C. Department of Health
    D. Department of Hospitals
    E. Department of Investigation

13. If, as the medical social worker in the voluntary hospital, you have known this woman and have been aware of her fear of surgery, the one of the following steps which would be BEST for you to take in order to help her in this transfer to a city hospital is to

    A. tell her that you will call the medical social worker in the city hospital who will help her during her stay there
    B. tell her that you will discuss her fears with the doctor at the city hospital
    C. promise to visit her at the city hospital and keep in touch with her
    D. tell her that the Department of Social Services investigator will visit her at the city hospital
    E. describe to her all the things which will be done during the surgery to allay her fears

14. When the Department of Social Services investigator hears of the patient's illness and hospitalization, the one of the following actions which he should take IMMEDIATELY is to

    A. close the case pending diagnosis
    B. notify the landlord not to hold the room
    C. recall any checks issued within the past ten days
    D. visit the patient in the hospital
    E. telephone the hospital for verification

14.____

15. Suppose the patient is to be discharged from the city hospital following surgery, but will need two or three months of nursing home care before she is able to return to living alone in a furnished room.
    The one of the following which will have to finance such nursing home care is the

    A. American Cancer Society
    B. Department of Social Services
    C. Ladies' Auxiliary of the city hospital
    D. patient's relatives or friends
    E. Department of Hospitals

15.____

Questions 16-17.

DIRECTIONS: Questions 16 and 17 are to be answered SOLELY on the basis of the facts given below.

CASE B

A 22-year-old pregnant woman was referred to medical social service by the nurse in the clinic of a city hospital. The nurse reported that the patient had cried following the examination which disclosed her pregnancy and, when questioned by the doctor, she said she was very distressed by her marital situation. You, as the medical social worker assigned to the case, learn that her husband is the superintendent of the house in which they live and that he receives free rent but no salary. He does odd jobs to earn money and buys groceries and other necessities, but will not give his wife any money. The husband drinks very heavily.

The patient says this is her second pregnancy. The first child, now 15 months old, was born five months after her marriage. She says she wants to leave her husband but wonders how she can support her babies. She would agree to stay with her husband if he would give her money.

16. On the basis of the facts given in Case B, the one of the following steps you would take is:

    A. Referral to the Department of Social Services
    B. Referral to a family agency
    C. Referral to Domestic Relations Court
    D. Discussion of the problem with the patient's husband
    E. Discussion of the problem with available relatives

16.____

17. As the patient described in Case B has no relatives, she is also concerned as to who will take care of her 15-month-old daughter during her confinement. 17.____
The one of the following suggestions which would be MOST helpful is that

    A. application be made to the child care division of the Department of Social Services
    B. her husband take over this responsibility
    C. a neighbor take the child into her home
    D. the child be taken to the Children's Shelter
    E. application be made to a family agency for homemaker service

Questions 18-20.

DIRECTIONS: Questions 18 through 20 are to be answered SOLELY on the basis of the facts given below.

CASE C

A woman, pregnant out of wedlock, in her 8th month of pregnancy, cones to you as the medical social worker in a city hospital, asking you to arrange for the adoption of her baby. She says she has no friends and is not interested in any plan for the baby other than adoption.

18. The one of the following agencies to which you would refer the woman described in Case C is the 18.____

    A. Spence-Chapin Adoption Service
    B. Bureau of Child Welfare of the Department of Social Services
    C. Surrogates' Court
    D. Domestic Relations Court
    E. Aid to Dependent Children Division of the Department of Social Services

19. The woman described in Case C is presently living in a furnished room and cannot pay the coming week's rent. She is Catholic and is willing to enter a shelter for unmarried mothers. 19.____
The one of the following shelters to which you would seek admission for her is

    A. The Wm. Booth Memorial Home and Hospital
    B. Inwood House
    C. The Heartsease Home for Women and Babies
    D. St. Faith's House
    E. The Guild of the Infant Saviour

20. When the baby is ready for adoption, the one of the following courts which would have jurisdiction over the adoption proceedings is the _____ Court. 20.____

    A. Criminal
    B. Surrogates'
    C. Family Division of Domestic Relations
    D. County
    E. Children's Court of Domestic Relations

KEY (CORRECT ANSWERS)

1.	C	11.	B
2.	A	12.	D
3.	A	13.	A
4.	B	14.	E
5.	D	15.	B
6.	B	16.	B
7.	E	17.	A
8.	A	18.	B
9.	C	19.	E
10.	D	20.	B

EXAMINATION SECTION
TEST 1

DIRECTIONS: Each question or incomplete statement is followed by several suggested answers or completions. Select the one that BEST answers the question or completes the statement. *PRINT THE LETTER OF THE CORRECT ANSWER IN THE SPACE AT THE RIGHT.*

1. A medical social worker can give service to an incurably ill patient MOST effectively by

    A. urging him to sleep and rest a great deal to conserve his strength
    B. helping him to gain what satisfaction he can within the limits imposed by his illness
    C. instructing his family to give him everything he asks for
    D. limiting her visits to him so she will not tire him

2. A SOUND motive for entering the field of social work is a desire to

    A. satisfy a personal need for giving
    B. be in a position to dispense charity
    C. accumulate information concerning the behavior of maladjusted people
    D. help people whose lives are unhappy or without satisfaction

3. The one of the following which is of MOST value to a social case worker in carrying out her functions in any field of social work is a(n)

    A. full knowledge of community resources
    B. totally objective viewpoint toward hostile behavior
    C. awareness of the purposeful use of relationships
    D. mature personality free from conflicts

4. The social case worker, in giving help to a client, should use PRIMARILY

    A. the community facilities available to meet needs
    B. the resources of the patient and his immediate environment
    C. the agency policies to determine her focus
    D. psychiatric concepts of human behavior

5. A case worker who is new to the field of social work will MOST probably focus her efforts PRIMARILY on

    A. the problem as presented by the client
    B. the client in relation to his problem
    C. developing self-awareness in handling clients
    D. the emotional needs of the client

6. A social worker who cannot adhere to agency policies is MOST likely to be a person who

    A. cannot relate to people
    B. has problems centered around questions of authority
    C. has deep feelings of guilt
    D. has many domestic problems

7. The one of the following cases which a beginning social case worker would probably find the LEAST difficult to handle is one involving a(n)

   A. juvenile delinquent
   B. enuretic child
   C. normal child in need of convalescent care
   D. stuttering child

8. A social worker can BEST begin to help a couple with a marital problem by FIRST

   A. referring them to a psychiatrist
   B. referring them to the family physician for guidance
   C. suggesting that they go to court with their problem
   D. helping them to clarify for themselves the nature of their problem

9. The social case worker often finds that legally responsible relatives of her clients are hostile when expected to contribute towards support or payment of medical expenses of the client.
   The one of the following which would be the MOST desirable way of dealing with such hostility is for the social worker to

   A. look into her own background to understand why these relatives are so resistant
   B. tell the relatives that this is a legal responsibility which cannot be evaded
   C. suggest that the relatives contact their legislators toward changing this requirement
   D. acknowledge the hardships involved for relatives and give understanding and treatment of the problem involved

10. A medical social work consultant from the Crippled Children's Bureau, in helping to set up a program of convalescent care for long-term orthopedically crippled patients, should prefer foster home care to institutional care PRIMARILY because

    A. a greater degree of emotional security would thereby be provided
    B. the children could then attend public school with normal children
    C. medical care of the children would then be better
    D. the families could then visit the children more frequently

11. The one of the following statements in regard to the emotional needs and attitudes of children which is MOST accurate is that

    A. it is not possible for a working mother to meet the emotional needs of her child
    B. parents who receive public assistance cannot meet the child's need for security
    C. a child who is emotionally secure does not have feelings of aggression
    D. parental support and acceptance are important to develop a feeling of belonging in the child

12. Persistent feeding problems with nursery or school-age children are MOST probably caused by 12.____

    A. hostility toward the mother
    B. the physical make-up of the child
    C. impoverished home conditions
    D. basic personality maladjustments

13. Local health departments and crippled children's agencies are assuming more and more responsibility for the teaching of various professional groups. Medical social workers are participating actively in programs of educational institutions and in-service training. The CHIEF objective of such teaching by a medical social worker is to 13.____

    A. supplement the knowledge of other professional groups so that they may perform minor case work services for the patient group
    B. teach social work concepts and demonstrate the need for more extensive medical social work
    C. encourage each professional group to realize fully the need of understanding every individual
    D. bring to other professions an approach to medical social work techniques which can be integrated into their own practice

14. The provision of medical services by the Department of Social Services for its recipients is presently and has been in the past 14.____

    A. focused on rehabilitation through employment
    B. all-inclusive to meet the needs of the clients
    C. supplementary to other community health services
    D. focused primarily on the medical needs of adults

15. Assume that a child who is a ward of the Foundling Hospital and who has been in a foster home placement through that agency is admitted to a city hospital with acute appendicitis. 15.____
    The required consent for an operation MUST be obtained from the

    A. hospital superintendent   B. foster parent
    C. Foundling Hospital   D. next of kin

16. The one of the following which is the MOST important point for a medical social worker to stress in the initial orientation of a group of new case workers to the use of agency case records is the 16.____

    A. statistical use of the records
    B. confidentiality of the material
    C. value of records in court
    D. type of recording used

17. When a medical social worker in a hospital is requested to assist with the teaching of medical students, it is a CARDINAL principle that the meetings must

    A. be attended by either the supervisor or the director of the social service division
    B. be held at the hospital to give meaning to the students
    C. be sponsored by the clinical teacher of the students
    D. have a patient present for demonstration purposes

17.____

18. An employee in a social agency who is charged with administrative functions should

    A. carry personal liability insurance
    B. make his opinions subordinate to those of his staff members
    C. be willing to delegate authority
    D. make decisions regarding all matters of policy without consulting his staff members

18.____

19. In interpreting agency function and administrative structure to a group of case workers, it is important to point out that policies are set up PRIMARILY to

    A. define the duties of each worker
    B. limit the amount of expenditures
    C. obtain state or federal reimbursement
    D. provide help for client and worker

19.____

20. Consultation in social work is MOST effective when the consultee

    A. understands that such consultation is an administrative order
    B. has a set schedule for consultation conferences
    C. recognizes his need for help and requests it
    D. recognizes the superior intelligence of the consultant

20.____

Questions 21-25.

DIRECTIONS: In Questions 21 through 25, Column I lists titles of books and Column II lists authors. Select the author for each book listed in Column I and write the letter which precedes the author in the blank space at the right, which corresponds to the number of the question.

COLUMN I

21. SUPERVISION IN SOCIAL CASE WORK
22. SOCIAL WELFARE AND PROFESSIONAL EDUCATION
23. SHADOW ON THE LAND; SYPHILIS
24. THE MEANING OF DISEASE
25. SOCIAL ASPECTS OF ILLNESS

COLUMN II

A. Edith Abbott
B. Carol Cooley
C. Thomas Parran
D. G. Canby Robinson
E. Virginia P. Robinson
F. Frances Upham
G. William A. White

21.____

22.____

23.____

24.____

25.____

KEY (CORRECT ANSWERS)

1.	B	11.	D
2.	D	12.	D
3.	C	13.	D
4.	B	14.	C
5.	A	15.	C
6.	B	16.	B
7.	C	17.	C
8.	D	18.	C
9.	D	19.	D
10.	A	20.	C

21. E
22. A
23. C
24. G
25. B

———

TEST 2

DIRECTIONS: Each question or incomplete statement is followed by several suggested answers or completions. Select the one that BEST answers the question or completes the statement. *PRINT THE LETTER OF THE CORRECT ANSWER IN THE SPACE AT THE RIGHT.*

1. The federal government accepts a responsibility for promoting and stimulating a comprehensive health program for all our people.
   The CHIEF reason for the assumption of this responsibility is that

   A. the health of our people is probably our most important national resource
   B. in some of the states the morbidity and mortality rates are extremely high
   C. greater medical needs are emerging as the nation is getting to be *a nation of elders*
   D. the medical profession has been unable to cover the needs of the major portion of the population

   1.____

2. The medical profession was at first opposed to state legislation calling for mandatory reporting by doctors of certain contagious and communicable diseases to local health departments.
   Their resistance was based PRIMARILY on the fact that they believed that

   A. this law would cause them to lose their patients
   B. the individual was more important than society
   C. this law was a violation of medical ethics
   D. this law would lead to socialized medicine

   2.____

3. The state governments in the United States have traditionally assumed responsibility for caring for

   A. merchant seamen
   B. the mentally ill
   C. patients with contagious diseases
   D. victims of industrial accidents

   3.____

4. The one of the following organizations which is supported from public funds is the

   A. National Institution of Health
   B. American Public Welfare Association
   C. American Public Health Association
   D. National Council on Family Relations

   4.____

5. Prior to 1935, the federal government assumed medical responsibility CHIEFLY for

   A. widows and orphans   B. federal employees
   C. tuberculous patients   D. military personnel

   5.____

6. The one of the following programs of the Social Security Act which is DIRECTLY administered by the federal government through the Social Security Administration is

   A. old age and survivors' insurance
   B. aid to the disabled
   C. aid to crippled children
   D. old age assistance

   6.____

7. The Social Security Act authorizes funds to be allotted by the Children's Bureau to the states so that needed services can be made readily available to all crippled children in the state.
In actual practice,

   A. the eligibility of a child for care is determined only on basis of medical needs
   B. states determine eligibility for service on basis of economic as well as medical needs
   C. all patients with childhood crippling conditions are accepted for care
   D. the act restricts the types of crippling conditions for which services will be available

8. The one of the following which would cause an employee to be INELIGIBLE for state unemployment insurance benefits is

   A. possession of a private unemployment insurance policy
   B. loss of job because of termination of business by employer
   C. dismissal because of seasonal layoffs
   D. dismissal because of misconduct

9. Old age and survivors' insurance and workmen's compensation are similar in that they both

   A. require a *means* test to determine eligibility for benefits
   B. are concerned with benefit rights based on past employment
   C. operate under state administration with federal guidance
   D. require court action for determination of benefits

10. In the city, shelter care for children is provided by private agencies as well as the Children's Center. The private agencies are licensed by the

    A. Department of Health
    B. Department of Welfare
    C. Department of Hospitals
    D. State Department of Social Services

11. The licensing of nursing homes in the city is the responsibility of the

    A. Department of Health
    B. Department of Hospitals
    C. Department of Social Services
    D. State Department of Social Welfare

12. A public welfare agency differs from a private welfare agency in that the former functions within

    A. administrative rules
    B. budgetary requirements
    C. a framework of law
    D. a wider geographical unit

13. Legal incorporation of a private social agency is IMPORTANT because

    A. members of the staff will then avoid personal responsibility for acts of the agency
    B. it results in greater efficiency in running the agency
    C. the agency can then solicit funds without restrictions
    D. no other agency can then be set up to carry out the same functions

14. The one of the following agencies which will cover the cost of nursing home visits to a relief recipient who is on the home care program of a city hospital is the

    A. Department of Hospitals
    B. Department of Social Services
    C. Nursing Sisters of the Sick Poor
    D. Visiting Nurse Service

15. If a child of 15 years is stricken with poliomyelitis and needs braces for which his family cannot pay, the braces can be obtained through the

    A. State Division of Vocational Rehabilitation
    B. Department of Social Services
    C. Department of Hospitals
    D. Department of Health

16. The one of the following statements which is MOST accurate in regard to the employability clinics of the Department of Social Services which are located in city hospitals is that

    A. the hospital is partially reimbursed for services rendered
    B. the Department of Social Services is able to use the facilities of the hospitals without any payment
    C. only treatment of minor ailments is available in these clinics
    D. laboratory services for the clinics are supplied by the Department of Health

17. The state will reimburse the city for the cost of hospitalization of a person receiving aid to the blind to the extent of _____ percent of the total cost.

    A. 30   B. 50   C. 80   D. 100

18. The one of the following services which is FALSE is that

    A. the Department of Social Services maintains a panel of full-time salaried physicians who devote their services to treatment of the recipients
    B. an adult, with his or her consent, may be legally adopted by another adult
    C. any client of the Department of Social Services requiring examination to determine the degree of blindness may be examined at a Department of Social Services eye clinic
    D. no minor should be treated in a hospital or clinic without written consent of a parent or guardian

19. The one of the following statements which is NOT true is that the Department of Social Services

    A. does not reimburse the Department of Hospitals for out-patient service given to its clients
    B. provides drugs for its clients who receive care in an out-patient clinic of a city hospital
    C. may provide appliances for a client attending an out-patient clinic of a city hospital
    D. will pay for a client's transportation to the outpatient clinic of a voluntary hospital

20. The one of the following statements in regard to the use of statistics in social work which is MOST valid is that

    A. statistics are non-essential to budget presentation
    B. statistics speak for themselves and need no interpretation
    C. uniformity of statistical controls is unimportant
    D. statistics are essential in planning the agency program

21. The one of the following which is the LEAST accurate statement in regard to the use of statistical controls in public welfare administration is that statistics

    A. furnish conclusive evidence as to the quality of the worker's performance
    B. are required by law
    C. are an indication of the employee's use of his time
    D. can serve as a supervisory tool for evaluation of work

22. The one of the following which is set up to further the control of alcoholism is

    A. Men's Shelter
    B. William Hodson Center
    C. Camp LaGuardia
    D. Bridge House

23. In the city, the administrative authority for carrying out the public program for physically handicapped children rests with the _____ Department of _____.

    A. city; Health
    B. city; Social Services
    C. city; Hospitals
    D. state; Social Services

24. Teaching case workers how to use community resources can BEST be done by

    A. group meetings
    B. planning field trips to several agencies
    C. relating the teaching to their own cases
    D. bringing speakers to the agency staff meetings

25. If a child of 17 whose family is receiving aid to dependent children needs orthodontia, this service will be provided by the Department of

    A. Education
    B. Hospitals
    C. Social Services
    D. Health

KEY (CORRECT ANSWERS)

1.	A	11.	B
2.	C	12.	C
3.	B	13.	A
4.	A	14.	A
5.	D	15.	D
6.	A	16.	B
7.	B	17.	B
8.	D	18.	A
9.	B	19.	B
10.	A	20.	D

21. A
22. D
23. A
24. C
25. D

TEST 3

DIRECTIONS: Each question or incomplete statement is followed by several suggested answers or completions. Select the one that BEST answers the question or completes the statement. *PRINT THE LETTER OF THE CORRECT ANSWER IN THE SPACE AT THE RIGHT.*

1. Assume that you are a medical social work consultant in the Department of Social Services, and a social investigator consults you about a client who refuses needed hospitalization. The investigator feels that the client should be pressured into accepting hospital care.
   The one of the following points which you should emphasize to the investigator is

   A. the desirability of getting relatives to sway the client towards accepting hospital care
   B. agency rules against the use of pressure
   C. the client's right of self-determination
   D. legal provisions against forcing the client to accept hospital care

2. The major part of the costs of medical care for persons receiving public assistance in the city is represented by

   A. hospital costs   B. physicians' visits
   C. nurses' visits   D. surgical appliances

3. The Public Health Law of the state was amended to change the provisions relating to charges and reimbursement for hospital care and treatment of persons with tuberculosis.
   The one of the following which is MOST accurate in regard to this amendment is that

   A. the state will reimburse each locality 100% for state charges in local tuberculosis hospitals
   B. the 50% state aid formula is changed to a maximum of $5 per patient day
   C. each locality is now responsible for the total cost of the care of its own residents in tuberculosis hospitals
   D. the state will assume full responsibility for the treatment and hospitalization of all diagnosed tuberculosis patients within the state

4. The services of a panel physician may not be authorized for clients of the Department of Social Services known to be suffering from

   A. an acute upper respiratory infection
   B. any contagious disease
   C. a chronic disease
   D. an acute form of venereal disease

5. In order to function most effectively as a medical social work consultant in the Department of Social Services, it would be important for the consultant to

   A. plan weekly conferences with the individual investigators around medical problems in their cases
   B. meet regularly on a scheduled basis with the unit supervisors to discuss cases with medical aspects
   C. review all the new cases each month for medical problems
   D. interview those clients who refuse to accept recommended medical care

35

6. In regard to the placement of clients of the Department of Social Services in nursing homes, the one of the following statements which is NOT true is that

   A. authorization by the medical director for nursing home care must be reviewed every three months
   B. assistance may be granted to residents of only those nursing homes which are approved by the Department of Social Services
   C. placement and residence in a nursing home must have the client's full consent and cooperation
   D. a plan for nursing home care requires the approval of the unit supervisor and the medical social work consultant

7. The medical care program in the Children's Center of the Department of Social Services is the direct responsibility of the Bureau of

   A. Child Welfare
   B. Social Services
   C. Institutional Administration
   D. Welfare Administration

Questions 8-11.

DIRECTIONS: Questions 8 through 11 are to be answered on the basis of the facts given in the case described below.

CASE I

Assume that you are a medical social work consultant in the Department of Social Services and a unit supervisor asks your assistance in the following case which is being carried by one of her investigators.

A young unmarried expectant mother from another city requests help with planning for herself and her baby. Except for one visit to a doctor to determine whether or not she was pregnant, she has had no prenatal care. She is without funds and has been evicted from her furnished room because of non-payment of rent. She is hesitant about giving information about herself because she does not wish her parents to know of her pregnancy. She has written to the father of her baby, who is a sergeant in the army, informing him of her pregnancy but has received no answer from him. She speaks vaguely of boarding the baby until she gets on her feet financially.

8. The one of the following which should be the social investigator's FIRST step in helping this girl is to

   A. offer her concrete help with her immediate problems, such as finding a place to live and planning for herself and her baby
   B. urge her to tell her parents so that they might help her
   C. discuss with her the advantages and disadvantages of boarding the baby or placing it for adoption
   D. offer to contact the baby's father through Red Cross

9. The one of the following agencies which would be LEAST likely to offer a helpful service to the client in this situation is the

   A. American Red Cross
   B. Department of Welfare
   C. St. Giles' Home
   D. Foundling Hospital

10. If this girl continues to be undecided about plans for her baby, the one of the following ways in which the social investigator could BEST help her is by

    A. suggesting that she get in touch with her parents so that she might have the benefit of their advice and counsel
    B. encouraging her to evaluate all possible plans and their advantages and disadvantages for the baby and for herself
    C. supporting her inclination to keep the baby and offering to help her find a foster home
    D. suggesting that she wait until she sees the baby before she considers plans

11. The one of the following ways in which the investigator could BEST help this girl to use this experience to make a more satisfactory adjustment to life in the future is by

    A. recognizing that she is lonely and referring her to recreational resources
    B. pointing out that unmarried mothers are neurotic and referring her to a psychiatrist
    C. helping her to use the interviews with the investigator to gain some self-understanding
    D. suggesting that the patient go home after the baby is born, since she appears to be unable to make a good adjustment away from her family and friends

Questions 12-20.

DIRECTIONS: Questions 12 through 20 are to be answered on the basis of the facts given in the case described below.

CASE II

Assume that in your capacity as a medical social work consultant in the Department of Social Services, the following situation is brought to your attention by a social investigator.

Mrs. G., a thirty-five year old Catholic woman, mother of three children and now pregnant, has been deserted by her husband and applies to the Department of Social Services for financial assistance. She says she does not know where her husband is. He had supported the family by working as a longshoreman until three months ago when he was discovered to have active tuberculosis. At that time, sanatorium care was recommended but he refused to go, and soon after he deserted his family.

Mrs. G. says her only living relatives are her step-mother, who lives with her, and two married step-brothers, living in the city, who have been helping her since Mr. G. deserted, but who now feel she should get help from the Department of Social Services. Mr. G.'s only relative is his mother, living in the city.

12. In abandoning his wife while she is pregnant, Mr. G. was LEGALLY guilty of

    A. a misdemeanor   B. a felony
    C. vagrancy   D. a fraud

13. The one of the following agencies which should be contacted FIRST in attempting to locate Mr. G. is the

    A. National Desertion Bureau
    B. Federal Bureau of Investigation
    C. Department of Social Services
    D. Police Department

14. If the Department of Social Services should be notified that Mr. G. is working in the city and able, but unwilling, to contribute to his family's support, the court where the department would start action is the ____ Court.

    A. Family Division of the Domestic Relations
    B. Children's Division of the Domestic Relations
    C. Criminal
    D. Supreme

15. If it is proved in this case that neither the father nor the mother is able to support the children, the LEGAL responsibility for the support of the children falls upon

    A. Mr. G.'s mother
    B. the Department of Social Services
    C. Mrs. G.'s step-mother
    D. Mrs. G.'s step-brothers

16. On the basis of Mrs. G.'s statement that her husband had active tuberculosis prior to his desertion, the social investigator on the case believes that each family member should be examined. The one of the following which would give DEFINITE evidence of active pulmonary tuberculosis in any of the family members is

    A. BCG vaccine   B. a Mantoux test
    C. a patch test   D. Roentgen study

17. The one of the following agencies to which you would refer the family for examination for tuberculosis is the

    A. nearest voluntary clinic
    B. State Tuberculosis and Health Association
    C. nearest city hospital
    D. Department of Health

18. If one of the children were found to have active pulmonary tuberculosis, the one of the following hospitals which would admit the child is ____ Hospital.

    A. St. Charles   B. Knickerbocker
    C. Seaview   D. Willowbrook

19. Mrs. G. shows concern about the care of her children during the period of her confinement. She states that if she goes to a hospital for delivery of her child, her step-mother would not be physically capable of giving them adequate care.
    In this situation, the one of the following plans which would be MOST adequate is to

    A. arrange home delivery
    B. plan for homemaker service
    C. place the children
    D. prove the step-mother's ability to care for the children

20. If Mrs. G. decides to go to a voluntary hospital clinic for prenatal care prior to delivery, the Department of Social Services will pay for

    A. medicines   B. laboratory fees
    C. x-ray examination   D. clinic fees

Questions 21-25.

DIRECTIONS: In Questions 21 through 25, Column I lists important happenings in the field of social welfare, and Column II lists dates. For each event listed in Column I, select its date from Column II, and write the letter which precedes the date in the space at the right corresponding to the number of the question.

	COLUMN I	COLUMN II	
21.	Enactment of the New York State Workmen's Compensation Law	A. 1875 B. 1910	21._____
22.	Enactment of the New York State Public Welfare Law	C. 1912 D. 1929	22._____
23.	Passage of the Social Security Act	E. 1931 F. 1933	23._____
24.	Establishment of the U.S. Children's Bureau	G. 1935	24._____
25.	Passage of the Federal Emergency Relief Act		25._____

KEY (CORRECT ANSWERS)

1. C
2. A
3. B
4. D
5. B

6. A
7. A
8. A
9. C
10. B

11. C
12. B
13. D
14. A
15. A

16. D
17. D
18. C
19. B
20. A

21. B
22. D
23. G
24. C
25. F

EXAMINATION SECTION
TEST 1

DIRECTIONS: Each question or incomplete statement is followed by several suggested answers or completions. Select the one that BEST answers the question or completes the statement. *PRINT THE LETTER OF THE CORRECT ANSWER IN THE SPACE AT THE RIGHT.*

1. The one of the following diseases which is the LEADING cause of death in the 10-to-15 year age group is
    A. cancer
    B. tuberculosis
    C. poliomyelitis
    D. diabetes
    E. rheumatic fever

    1.____

2. The one of the following which would MOST likely be a result of untreated syphilis is
    A. paresis
    B. phlebitis
    C. carcinoma
    D. silicosis
    E. angina pectoris

    2.____

3. The one of the following which is MOST likely to be used in establishing a diagnosis of epilepsy is a(n)
    A. electrocardiogram
    B. spinal x-ray
    C. fluoroscopic examination
    D. electroencephalogram
    E. psychometric examination

    3.____

4. The pathology of diabetes involves the FAILURE of the body to produce an adequate supply of
    A. sugar
    B. carbohydrates
    C. insulin
    D. salt
    E. bile

    4.____

5. The one of the following statements that is TRUE about diabetes is that
    A. it can generally be cured if medical orders are followed
    B. it can generally be kept under control but not cured
    C. it is an infectious disease
    D. blindness is an inevitable result of it
    E. controlled diabetes is a progressively disabling disease

    5.____

6. Scurvy is caused by a deficiency of vitamin
    A. A
    B. B
    C. C
    D. E
    E. K

    6.____

7. Vitamin D deficiency is common because
    A. it can only be injected
    B. it is generally associated with poorly tasting foods
    C. only physicians can administer it
    D. it is not found naturally in many foods

    7.____

8. The one of the following vitamins that is used as an aid in coagulating blood is vitamin
    A. A
    B. B
    C. C
    D. E
    E. K

    8.____

9. The one of the following statements that is TRUE of Duchenne muscular dystrophy is that
    A. it is transmitted to the male children through the mother
    B. the male is the carrier of the disease
    C. the brain is primarily affected because of a lack of blood supply
    D. it is caused by a nutritional deficiency in the antepartum period
    E. only female children are susceptible to the disease

10. If a patient is repeatedly admitted to the hospital because of a series of mishaps in which he has suffered broken bones, the one of the following that is MOST likely to be true is that he is
    A. a rigid person   B. a diabetic   C. malingering
    D. accident prone   E. psychotic

11. The one of the following groups of illnesses that is known to be caused by bacteria is
    A. mental diseases   B. acute infectious diseases
    C. nutritional diseases   D. degenerative diseases
    E. cancerous tumors

12. The one of the following with which Hodgkin's Disease is COMMONLY associated is
    A. neurasthenia   B. meningitis   C. poliomyelitis
    D. cancer   E. tuberculosis

13. The one of the following diseases in which the determination of the sedimentation rate is IMPORTANT for diagnostic purposes is
    A. rheumatic heart disease   B. congenital heart disease
    C. hypertensive heart disease   D. diabetes
    E. gonorrhea

14. The one of the following disease classifications that would INCLUDE spinal meningitis is
    A. cancer or tumor   B. nutritional disease
    C. acute infectious disease   D. focal or local infection
    E. acute poisoning or intoxication

15. The one of the following diseases that may cause visual impairment and blindness is
    A. ringworm   B. osteomyelitis
    C. poliomyelitis   D. gall bladder disease
    E. diabetes

16. The one of the following that is NOT an anesthetic is
    A. cholesterol   B. nitrous oxide   C. sodium pentothal
    D. procaine   E. ethyl chloride

17. The one of the following that BEST describes the restrictions to be applied to Mr. K., a cardiac patient classified, according to the standards of the American Heart Association, as functional, Class IVD, is
    A. limited activity
    B. complete bed rest
    C. four hours rest daily
    D. prohibition of stair climbing, alcohol or tobacco
    E. convalescent status

18. Over time, geriatrics has become an increasingly important branch of medicine CHIEFLY due to
    A. greater specialization within the medical profession
    B. the discovery of penicillin and aureomycin
    C. advances in medical education
    D. increases in hospitalization
    E. the increase in the span of life

19. The one of the following which is MOST likely to be an occupational disease is
    A. cancer   B. cerebral hemorrhage
    C. septicemia   D. asthma
    E. nephritis

20. The one of the following that is a NUTRITIONAL disease is
    A. tuberculosis   B. scurvy   C. hepatitis
    D. lymphoma   E. scabies

21. Morbidity rate refers to the
    A. incidence of an illness
    B. ratio of births to deaths
    C. bacterial count
    D. degree of disability caused by an illness
    E. death rate

22. A pediatrician is a doctor who specializes in the treatment of
    A. children   B. foot diseases
    C. disabling illnesses   D. orthopedic diseases
    E. the aged

23. A sadistic person is one who
    A. receives gratification through suffering pain
    B. secures a great deal of satisfaction from his own body
    C. receives gratification from inflicting pain on others
    D. turns all feelings towards others back into his own personality
    E. seeks solace through deep mental depression

24. The one of the following which is said to be the masculine counterpart of the *Electra Complex* is the _____ complex.
    A. sexual perversion   B. frustration   C. Oedipus
    D. reanimation   E. repression

25. The one of the following conditions for which a patient would be admitted to a state mental hospital is
    A. schizophrenia
    B. muscular dystrophy
    C. pathological lying
    D. congenital syphilis
    E. psychoneurosis

26. The one of the following statements which BEST describes the difference between a hallucination and a delusion is that
    A. hallucinations occur only at night
    B. delusions occur only with menopause
    C. delusions are primarily provoked by sexual function
    D. a hallucination has a basis in beliefs or ideas
    E. a delusion has a basis in beliefs or ideas

27. Finger sucking in early childhood has long been a subject of discussion among psychiatrists.
    The one of the following statements that is GENERALLY accepted as true is that
    A. finger sucking denotes pending neuroses and the parents need psychiatric consultation
    B. finger sucking is a normal activity of early childhood and should not be interfered with
    C. finger sucking alters the child's facial contours and should be heavily discouraged
    D. finger sucking by a child over nine months old is due to emotional upset and needs treatment
    E. the physician should discuss possible remedial measures such as guards on fingers

28. The one of the following who is said to be the *Father of Medicine* is
    A. Hippocrates   B. Pasteur   C. Galen
    D. Sydenham   E. Plato

29. The one of the following who is credited with the improvement of conditions in mental hospitals and the founding of new ones in the United States is
    A. Andrew Jackson
    B. Dorothea Dix
    C. William Knowlton
    D. Robert Stack
    E. Rene Laennec

30. The one of the following doctors whose name is COMMONLY associated with much of the early growth and subsequent progress of medical social work is Dr.
    A. Sigmund Freud
    B. Richard C. Cabot
    C. Elizabeth Blackwell
    D. Carmyn Lombardo
    E. Thomas Parran

KEY (CORRECT ANSWERS)

1.	A	11.	B	21.	A
2.	A	12.	D	22.	A
3.	D	13.	A	23.	C
4.	C	14.	C	24.	C
5.	B	15.	E	25.	A
6.	C	16.	A	26.	E
7.	D	17.	B	27.	B
8.	E	18.	E	28.	A
9.	A	19.	D	29.	B
10.	D	20.	B	30.	B

EXAMINATION SECTION
TEST 1

DIRECTIONS: Each question or incomplete statement is followed by several suggested answers or completions. Select the one that BEST answers the question or completes the statement. *PRINT THE LETTER OF THE CORRECT ANSWER IN THE SPACE AT THE RIGHT.*

1. As a worker in the out-patient clinic, you are helping a patient complete a Medicaid application. Although he appears to be eligible, the patient is reluctant to give the information necessary to complete the application.
   Of the following, your MOST appropriate action in this situation would be to

   A. inform your supervisor that the patient is uncooperative and request permission to close the case
   B. advise the patient that he can not be seen in the clinic again unless the application is completed
   C. discuss with the patient the reasons for his reluctance to apply for medical assistance
   D. explain to the patient that the bill will be turned over to a collection agency if the Medicaid application is not completed

2. You are interviewing a middle-aged man who is depressed about having to be in the hospital for a medical emergency at this particular time, when his wife and children are away. You once had a similar personal experience, and managed to handle your feelings of loneliness and depression successfully.
   When the man finishes his story, *which one* of the following would be your most appropriate FIRST response?

   A. Tell the man how you handled your situation and suggest that he use the same approach
   B. Tell the man you know just how he feels and are sympathetic
   C. Suggest that, if he gets a good night's sleep, he will feel better in the morning
   D. Tell the man how you handled your situation, and explore with him his feelings about trying the same approach

3. As a worker on the pediatric service, you receive a phone call from a woman who reports that her neighbor's six-month-old infant has black and blue marks all over its body. She states that she has heard sounds from the neighbor's apartment that make her suspect the child has been beaten.
   Of the following, your MOST appropriate response to this call would be to

   A. refer the woman to central registry of special services for children, explaining that the agency will investigate and that her report will be confidential
   B. advise the woman that you cannot take action on the basis of a phone call but that she should come in to see you personally about the matter
   C. inform the woman that it is poor practice to become involved in the domestic affairs of neighbors
   D. tell the woman to contact the police and have the parents investigated and possibly arrested for child abuse

4. You have been counseling a long-term patient once a week for several weeks. However, due to a reorganization in your hospital's department of social work, this patient will be assigned to another worker within three weeks. Of the following, the MOST appropriate time to tell the patient about the change in workers is

   A. immediately to give you time to help the patient adjust to the idea of another worker
   B. at the time of the new worker's first visit, to avoid any possible resentment by the patient towards you
   C. at the beginning of your final visit, to allow time to tell the patient what you know about the new worker
   D. at the end of your final visit, to avoid a possible sentimental farewell scene

4.____

5. As a worker assigned to the psychiatric walk-in-clinic, you receive a phone call from a man who says that his wife has just swallowed 20 sleeping pills, after an argument. Of the following, your MOST appropriate action would be to

   A. advise the man to calm down because this is probably not a lethal dose
   B. tell the man to give his wife large quantities of black coffee and walk her around so that she does not become unconscious
   C. offer the man an emergency appointment in the marital counseling clinic
   D. instruct the man to get immediate emergency medical assistance for his wife

5.____

6. As you enter the clinic area where you are assigned as a worker, you see an elderly man trip and fall on the curb near the doorway. Which one of the following actions should you take FIRST?

   A. Inform the executive director about this accident
   B. Assist the man to his feet and help him into the clinic area so that he can be more comfortable
   C. Stay with the man and tell him not to move while you ask someone to summon help
   D. Go to the nearest phone and call the police

6.____

7. Assume that a client is telling you the details of her previous surgery, including her problems during after-care treatment and the reactions of her family members towards her treatment. Since she will shortly undergo another similar operation, she is anxious to avoid some of the problems she had the last time.
The number of written notes you should take while this patient is talking should be

   A. *extensive,* due to the considerable detail and complexity of the discussion
   B. *minimal,* since this discussion demands your full attention, and notes can be written after the interview
   C. *extensive,* so that the client will feel that her problems are of extreme importance
   D. *minimal,* since complete notes should be taken immediately after this discussion but before ending the interview

7.____

8. You are interviewing a patient for the second time and you find that your relationship with him is becoming rather strained, which of the following would be the BEST way to handle this situation? Consider this development to be

   A. *routine,* and review your own attitudes and actions towards the client during your first interview, and the content of the interview
   B. *unusual,* and analyze the client's personality for reasons for the negative reaction
   C. *routine,* and ask your supervisor to assign this case to another worker
   D. *unusual,* and ask the client to explain possible reasons for his hostility

8.____

9. Mrs. Heeney, a 58-year-old former out-patient of the diabetic clinic, was doing well with the use of oral medication for several years, but has required daily injectitons of insulin during the past year. However, she finds It difficult to give herself injections, despite instruction at the clinic, and as a result has been hospitalized for diabetic shock for the second time. The doctors ask you to see what can be done to help Mrs. Heeney. Of the following, your FIRST action should be to

   A. schedule a psychiatric evaluation and recommend therapy to help Mrs. Heeney overcome her fears
   B. talk with Mr. Heeney to see whether he would be willing to give his wife the daily injections
   C. tell Mrs. Heeney she will be kept in the hospital until she learns and is able to give herself the injections
   D. enlist Mrs. Heeney's cooperation in learning to give herself injections in the hospital and then at home with the help of a visiting nurse

9.____

10. Mrs. Dean, a waitress, age 24, has been seen in the Emergency Room for the second time in ten days as a result of on-the-job accidents. She has told the doctor that she is tired and tense all the time and is unable to concentrate on what she is doing at her job. The doctor has referred her to both the medical clinic and social services for further work-ups.
As the worker assigned to this case, of the following, the most advisable way to handle this case INITIALLY would be to

   A. ask for a report on the completed medical work-up before interviewing Mrs. Dean, in order to be aware of any medical conditions which might be affecting her fatigue and tenseness
   B. interview Mrs. Dean during the period in which she is underoing the medical work-up, in order to determine whether there are any psycho-social factors contributing to her condition
   C. interview Mrs. Dean during the period in which she is undergoing the medical work-up, and recommend psychiatric consultation at the same time
   D. refer Mrs. Dean for a psychological evaluation, and schedule your preliminary interview after you have received a report on the evaluation

10.____

11. The clinic doctor has asked you to speak with Ms. Farley because she frequently breaks clinic appointments, which the doctor considers dangerous in light of her serious medical condition. During the interview, you find that Ms. Farley seems to be more concerned about her housing and welfare problems than her medical condition.
Of the following, the BEST way to handle this situation would be to

   A. tell Ms. Farley to discuss her housing and welfare problems directly with those agencies, because it is more important for the hospital social worker to help her with her medical problems
   B. tell Ms. Farley that you would like to help her with these other matters, but you think her health and medical care are of primary importance and should come first
   C. explore with Ms. Farley the nature and extent of her housing and welfare problems in order to see how you can be of help to her, deferring immediate discussion of her broken appointments
   D. tell her you will be glad to discuss her other problems with her, but only after you have first worked out and settled the matter of her broken medical appointments

11.____

12. You are asked to look into the case of William T., age 9, who was referred to the pediatric clinic by his school principal because he is inattentive and falls asleep in class. The pediatrician finds no medical basis for these problems. As the result of a home visit, you find that there is continual quarreling between his parents, which is having a bad effect on William and his two younger brothers. The father has been unemployed for six months.
Of the following, your BEST course of action would be to

    A. refer the case to special services for children as a suspected case of child neglect
    B. seek to place William T. and his brothers in a foster home until the parents can resolve their problems
    C. offer to help Mr. T. get a job and consider the possibility of obtaining a second medical opinion regarding William's inattentiveness and sleepiness
    D. ask your supervisor to consider whether the social worker should be assigned to make a fuller intra-familial assessment of this case

12.____

13. Mrs. Ware is the sole support of herself and her 9-year-old son, who is hospitalized for an orthopedic condition which requires a body cast from chest to ankles. The child will be ready to be discharged in two weeks, but will have to remain in the case for another three months and visit the clinic weekly. The ward team has asked you to see Mrs. Ware in order to plan for the discharge.
Of the following, the MOST appropriate way to advise Mrs. Ware during this interview would be to

    A. recommend that she take her vacation time or a leave of absence in order to care for her child
    B. suggest that the best thing she can do is place her son in a rehabilitation center so that she can go on working
    C. tell her that she should quit her job and go on unemployment insurance until her son is out of the cast
    D. work with her to help her arrive at what she feels would be best for both herself and her child

13.____

14. Ronald P., age 5, has a chronic condition for which he receives oral medication to be taken 4 times daily. Although this medication is effective in 90% of known cases, Ronald is usually out of control and requires emergency room care at least once a week. Mrs. P. says Ronald is given his medication regularly. However, during your discussion with the doctor on this case, he questions Mrs. P's reliability in giving Ronald the medication.
Of the following, the BEST way for you to handle this situation initially would be to

    A. have Mrs. P. keep a daily record of when she gives Ronald the medication and return this record to you in two weeks
    B. discuss this problem with the boy's father and ask him to make sure that the child is getting the medication regularly
    C. interview Mr. and Mrs. P. together at home, so that you can evaluate the family situation and any other factors which may relate to this problem
    D. suggest to the doctor that Ronald be hospitalized for a suitable period of time in order to determine definitely whether he can be controlled with regular medication

14.____

15. Mrs. Jurado's husband has been a patient on the medical ward for a week. Visiting hours are from 2-4 p.m. and 7-8 p.m. Mrs. Jurado comes daily shortly before 4 p.m. and usually leaves about 5:30 p.m. The nurses have been flexible but cannot continue to allow this, and ask you, the worker on the ward, to talk to Mrs. Jurado.
Of the following, you should ask the nurses to

   A. continue to be flexible about visiting hours with Mrs. Jurado, since it would be difficult to make her understand hospital policy.
   B. remain Mrs. flexible a day or two longer, until you help Jurado understand hospital policy on visiting hours
   C. restrict Mrs. Jurado to regular visiting hours, and let you know if she refuses, so that you can talk to her at that time
   D. restrict Mrs. Jurado to regular hours and explain the reasons to her themselves, since enforcing visiting hours is their responsibility

16. Which one of the following health service systems would generally be suitable for a chronically ill or disabled patient who has had an acute episode or a relapse at home?

   A. Skilled nursing home
   B. General hospital
   C. Extended care facility
   D. Home attendant service

17. Assume that you are trying to arrange placement for an elderly patient who, upon discharge from the hospital, will be able to get around and manage by herself, but will require some supervision.
Of the following, the MOST appropriate placement for this patient would be in a

   A. nursing home
   B. rehabilitation center
   C. chronic care facility
   D. health-related facility

18. Assume that one of your clients, a married woman with two small children, is in the hospital for a serious operation that will require a long-term stay. Her husband is regularly employed during the day.
Of the following, the MOST appropriate arrangement for care of this couple's children would be

   A. a foster home
   B. day care service
   C. homemaker service
   D. group home placement

19. Assume that you are helping an elderly patient with discharge planning. This patient, who is expected to live alone in his own apartment, will need around-the-clock assistance with personal needs, such as bathing and taking of medication.
Of the following services, the ONE that should be recommended for this patient is a

   A. homemaker
   B. housekeeper
   C. home attendant
   D. visiting nurse

20. The type of residence which provides an interim living and working experience in the transition from psychiatric hospital care to return to the community is commonly known as a

   A. rehabilitation center
   B. halfway house
   C. psychiatric clinic
   D. temporary day care facility

KEY (CORRECT ANSWERS)

1. C
2. D
3. A
4. A
5. D

6. C
7. B
8. A
9. D
10. B

11. C
12. D
13. D
14. D
15. B

16. B
17. D
18. C
19. C
20. B

TEST 2

DIRECTIONS: Each question or incomplete statement is followed by several suggested answers or completions. Select the one that *BEST* answers the question or completes the statement. *PRINT THE LETTER OF THE CORRECT ANSWER IN THE SPACE AT THE RIGHT.*

1. During an interview, you learn that a patient needs services from another agency. Of the following, the BEST way to make a referral for services from this agency is to

    A. call the agency to advise them that you are referring your client for services
    B. instruct the client to contact the agency and have the client fill out the required forms in advance
    C. write a referral letter to the agency explaining the client's problems and needs, and have the client bring it to the agency
    D. send the agency a release of information signed by the client and a summary of the client's problems, and request an appointment for the client

    1.____

2. You are counselling an elderly woman who lives alone. You and the doctor have decided that she requires nursing home placement upon discharge from the hospital. However, the woman has expressed fear and concern about being uprooted from her home and living among strangers.
In this situation, the BEST of the following courses of action would be to

    A. try to convince the woman that a nursing home is best
    B. allow the woman to make her own decision, after offering her advice and guidance
    C. recommend that the woman be permitted to live in her own home and manage as best she can
    D. ask the woman's doctor to encourage her to accept nursing home placement

    2.____

3. You are counselling Mrs. Andujar, a Spanish-speaking woman with limited ability to speak English, who was told by the pediatrician that no medical reason has been found for her child's abnormal behavior, and was referred to the child psychiatric clinic. However, after a month, Mrs. Andujar tells you that the child's behavior is worse and that she still doesn't have an appointment at the child psychiatric clinic. You discover that Mrs. Andujar has not returned the forms sent to her by the clinic.
Of the following, the BEST way to handle this situation is to

    A. tell Mrs. Andujar that nothing can be done until she completes the forms and returns them to the clinic
    B. send Mrs. Andujar to the clinic to explain her predicament to the social worker on that service
    C. help Mrs. Andujar complete the forms and ask the psychiatric clinic social worker to suggest the best way to expedite an appointment
    D. tell the pediatrician about Mrs. Andujar's difficulty with the forms as well as the child's condition and ask him to insist on an immediate clinic appointment

    3.____

4. Arleen, age 7, has recovered from her illness and will soon be discharged from the hospital. She has had many difficult experiences in her young life. Her father deserted the family last year, and her mother, with whom she was very close, died six months ago. Since then, Arleen has been living with her grandmother, who is elderly and ill, and cannot continue to care for her. You and the grandmother have decided together that foster

    4.____

53

home placement is essential for Arleen's well being, A referral has been accepted by special services for Children, and placement is anticipated in about two weeks. According to good social work practice, of the following, it would be MOST appropriate for you to

A. ask Arleen whether she would be willing to live apart from her grandmother in a nice new home
B. inform Arleen that she will be going to a nice home where she will be happy and have many new friends
C. tell Arleen, with the participation of her grandmother, of the plan for placement and the reasons for it, giving her every opportunity to express her feelings
D. advise Arleen of the plan for placement and the reasons for it, encouraging her to be brave no matter how sad she feels living apart from her grandmother

Questions 5-7.

DIRECTIONS: Answer Questions 5 through 7 based on the information given in the following case record.

Laura Jackson
Age: 52
Single
Parents: Deceased
Siblings: Sister – Sally Mays, age 53, married
Diagnosis: Multiple Sclerosis

Ms. Jackson, a high school graduate, supported herself as a sales clerk since graduation, but continued to live at home with her parents until their sudden death in an automobile accident 13 years ago. Since that time, she lived alone, but had continual contact with her older sister, Mrs. Sally Mays. A year ago, Ms. Jackson's hand became too unsteady for her to work. This condition had been preceded by forgetfulness and frequent mistakes. Examinations resulted in a diagnosis of multiple sclerosis and she became increasingly incapacitated until she had difficulty feeding and dressing herself. After a very serious fall, Ms. Jackson was hospitalized. The case worker, together with Mrs. Mays, arranged for Ms. Jackson to be placed in a nursing home in anticipation of her discharge from the hospital. She would be unable to care for herself alone at home, and her sister could not take care of her, because of household responsibilities. Ms. Jackson is extremely unhappy and angry when she is told about the decision to place her in a nursing home. She accuses her sister of plotting to put her away. Mrs. Mays turns to the case worker for advice.

5. On the basis of the information given above, of the following, the circumstance which would help explain Ms. Jackson's anger when she was told about being placed in a nursing home is that she

A. is probably becoming paranoid as a result of her illness
B. has undoubtedly actively disliked her sister for years
C. was not involved in the process of making the decision
D. was a dependent person before she became ill

6. When Mrs. Mays turns to the case worker for advice after recognizing her sister's anger, of the following, it would be MOST appropriate for the case worker to FIRST

A. *reassure* Mrs. Mays that she has made the best decision for Ms. Jackson's care
B. *tell* Mrs. Mays that you will visit Ms, Jackson and calm her down

C. *help* Mrs. Mays to understand why Ms. Jackson is upset
D. *ask* Mrs. Mays to visit Ms. Jackson and explain why the decision was made

7. Of the following, the *MOST* important factor to consider in finding a nursing home for Ms. Jackson is

    A. the ratio of men to women among the patients
    B. a location that will make it possible for Mrs. Mays to visit frequently
    C. her need for a single room, since she has always lived alone
    D. the average age of the other patients

Questions 8-10.

DIRECTIONS: Answer Questions 8 through 10 based on the information given in the following case record.

Joan Drew
Age: 40
Single
Children: Tom 8, Rose 6
Diagnosis: Paralysis of entire left side due to a stroke Ms. Drew, who dropped out of school in the eleventh grade, has had a variety of jobs in factories, as an elevator operator, and as a domestic. She now receives public assistance. In June, 2016, she was operated on for removal of her right kidney and for a hysterectomy. In November, 2017, she had a cerebro-vascular accident; diagnosis: hemiparesis left. In January, 2018, she had a cystoscopy operation.
After discharge in November, 2018, Ms. Drew was scheduled for weekly visits to the hospital's physical therapy clinic for treatment of her paralysis. To date she has continued her therapy faithfully and is now able to walk with a cane. However, her left hand and part of her arm have not responded well to treatment.
Ms. Drew's attitude is poor when she discusses her situation with the case worker. She feels that she will never recover because she is being punished for past wrong-doing. At times she feels persecuted by her doctors and others. She worries about her children; this appears to be unfounded, as they are healthy and doing well in school.

8. Ms. Drew's medical problems are described above in terms that would be used in a medical report. Of the following, the *MOST* important reason why the case worker should understand the meaning of these terms is to

    A. make it possible for doctors to include you in discussions of the patient
    B. improve your understanding of the patient's symptoms
    C. help you to sound like a professional at interdisciplinary meetings
    D. help your prospects for advancement in the medical social work field

9. The case worker should understand that Ms. Drew's fear that she is being punished for past wrong-doing is a problem that should be

    A. discussed with the supervisor for possible referral for psychiatric evaluation
    B. handled by psychiatric treatment
    C. treated by strong reassurance that she is not being punished for her sins
    D. considered to be an indication of psychotic behavior

10. Of the following, the underlying reason for Ms, Drew's exaggerated concerns about her children are probably the result of   10.____

    A. her fears about her own health and her future ability to care for her children
    B. her realization that she has made serious mistakes in bringing her children up
    C. her dependence upon her children to give her a sense of self-worth
    D. her desire to give her children more advantages and comforts than she had

Questions 11-14.

DIRECTIONS: Answer Questions 11 through 14 based SOLELY on the formation contained in the following passage.

After conducting and completing an interview, the interviewer is faced with the responsibility of recording it in some manner. Very considerable amounts of staff time and agency finances are absorbed in recording. Time and cost studies of agency expenditures indicate that, for every dollar spent on interviewing, three dollars are spent on recording. In addition to actual time spent by the worker in recording, such expense involves clerical transcribing time, filing time and space, and time in reading records.

Recording insures a continuity of client-agency contact that transcends the client's contact with any individual social worker. The case record also implements the agency's accountability to the community. It provides a permanent, documented account of services to clients. The interviewer about to record the interview faces the essential question, what should be recorded and how should the recording be organized? Just as purpose guides interview interaction, so it guides selection of material for recording. Traditionally, social work recording has been designed to meet a number of different purposes. We record to achieve more effective practice, to provide material for in-service training and teaching, and for research purposes. There is no consensus on the principal purpose of social work recording. Consequently, recording has served these various purposes with limited effectiveness, and has served no one purpose well.

11. According to the above passage, the relationship between recording and interviewing costs for social work purposes is such that   11.____

    A. recording is *three times* more expensive than interviewing
    B. recording is *one-third* as expensive as interviewing
    C. recording is *four times* more expensive than interviewing
    D. interviewing is *much more* expensive than recording

12. The *one* of the following that is SPECIFICALLY mentioned as a purpose of case recording is   12.____

    A. saving time   B. economy
    C. research   D. convenience

13. Of the following, according to the passage, a MAJOR contributing factor to the expense of case recording is   13.____

    A. supervision   B. in-service training
    C. research   D. record reading time

14. It can be concluded that the author's opinion regarding the capacity of social work recording to achieve its various purposes is   14.____

    A. enthusiastic   B. guarded   C. neutral   D. confused

Questions 15-17.

DIRECTIONS: Answer Questions 15 through 17 based SOLELY on the information contained in the following passage.

On the State level, in an effort to obtain better administration and delivery of services in the Medicaid program, the Governor has appointed a committee to advise the State Commissioner of Social Welfare on medical care services. Included on this committee are representatives of the medical, dental, pharmaceutical, nursing, and social work professions, as well as persons representing the fields of mental health, home health agencies, nursing homes, schools of health science, public health and welfare administrations, and the general public. Several of the committee members are physicians in private practice who represent and uphold the interests of the private physicians who care for Medicaid patients.

The committee not only makes recommendations on the standards, quality and costs of medical services, personnel, and facilities, but also helps identify unmet needs, and assists in long-range planning, evaluation and utilization of services. It advises, as requested, on administrative and fiscal matters, and also interprets the programs and goals to professional groups.

On the City level, representatives of the county medical societies of New York City meet periodically with Medicaid administrators to discuss problems and consider proposals. It is hoped that the county medical societies will assume the responsibility of informing citizens as to where they can receive medical care under Medicaid.

15. Based on information in the above passage, it can be inferred that the group on the advisory committee likely to be LEAST objective in their recommendations would be the representatives of the

   A. public health and welfare administrations
   B. general public
   C. private physicians
   D. schools of health science

16. The above passage suggests that a problem with the Medicaid program in New York City is that

   A. the Mayor has not appointed a committee to work with the City Commissioner of Social Services
   B. many people do not know where they can go to obtain medical care under the program
   C. the county medical societies of New York City do not meet often enough with the Medicaid program administrators
   D. citizens do not take the initiative to seek out sources of available medical care under the program

17. According to the above passage, the Governor's objective in appointing the advisory committee was to

   A. obtain more cooperation from the New York City county medical societies
   B. get the members of the committee to provide medical care services to Medicaid recipients
   C. help improve the Medicaid program in all its aspects, including administration and provision of services
   D. persuade a greater number of private physicians and other health care professionals to accept Medicaid patients

18. Which one of the following is the MOST desirable method of recording an interview with a client?

    A. Record sufficient detail to provide the reader with an understanding of the client's situation and needs
    B. Record as much detail as possible to minimize the necessity of relying on memory later
    C. Quote the key points made by the client to avoid potential misunderstanding and embarrassment
    D. Take very few notes and record as much as you can remember upon completion of the interview

19. Assume that you are preparing to write a case summary giving the essential information pertaining to the facts of a case clearly and briefly. Of the following, the MOST appropriate form to use for recording this type of information would be a

    A. process record
    B. discharge planning report
    C. case folder
    D. face sheet

20. The one of the following records which would be MOST useful in helping to develop a treatment plan for a patient is the

    A. face sheet
    B. medical service order
    C. social service medical record
    D. psycho-social summary

KEY (CORRECT ANSWERS)

1.	D	11.	A
2.	A	12.	C
3.	C	13.	D
4.	C	14.	B
5.	C	15.	C
6.	C	16.	B
7.	B	17.	C
8.	B	18.	A
9.	A	19.	D
10.	A	20.	D

EXAMINATION SECTION
TEST 1

DIRECTIONS: Each question or incomplete statement is followed by several suggested answers or completions. Select the one that *BEST* answers the question or completes the statement. *PRINT THE LETTER OF THE CORRECT ANSWER IN THE SPACE AT THE RIGHT.*

1. Generally, the *MAIN* reason for using the questioning technique in a case work interview is to

    A. reveal discrepancies in information given by the client
    B. reinforce your own ideas about the case
    C. obtain necessary factual information about the client
    D. bring out the hidden motives of the client

2. According to a basic case work principle, a worker should "accept" the client, regardless of the client's feelings, attitudes and behavior. This concept of "acceptance" means, most nearly, that the worker

    A. agrees with what the client says, does, and feels
    B. demonstrates his respect for the client as a human being
    C. has no strong opinions about the client's values
    D. thinks the way the client thinks

3. Before visiting a new client, it is desirable for you to be prepared in advance, when possible.
   Which one of the following should generally NOT be included in these advance preparations?

    A. *Learning* as much as possible about the client from the medical chart
    B. *Trying* to put yourself in the client's place
    C. *Recognizing* your own prejudices and stereotypes
    D. *Deciding* on a solution to the client's problems

4. After introducing yourself to a new patient, which one of the following questions generally would be the *MOST* appropriate for you to ask?

    A. "Do you expect any visitors today?"
    B. "Who is your attending physician?"
    C. "How can I be of help to you?"
    D. "Do you have hospitalization insurance?"

5. In the middle of an interview, a patient makes a statement which seems unclear. Of the following, the *BEST* way to deal with this situation would be for the worker to

    A. ask the patient to rephrase her statement
    B. rephrase the statement, and ask the patient if that is what she meant
    C. inform the patient that she is not making herself clear
    D. let the patient finish and then try to tie the story together

6. Assume that, at the conclusion of an interview with a client, you have reviewed problems that have been resolved. Generally, the MOST appropriate of the following closing actions for you to take would be to

   A. remind the patient to be on time for the next appointment
   B. go over specific actions that you and the client will take before the next visit
   C. remind the client to take tranquilizers when feeling upset
   D. ask the client to think of new problems to discuss during the next visit

7. Which one of the following would be a MAJOR responsibility of a worker assigned to the surgery ward?

   A. *Instructing* the nurse about changes in medication for patients
   B. *Advising* relatives of the best time to visit patients
   C. *Detecting* anxiety of patients due to their medical illness
   D. *Recording* the number of visitors received by patients

8. Assume that you have been assigned the case of an eight-year-old child whose parents were both seriously injured in an automobile accident. You realize that this child will have severe problems in the months ahead.
   During the *first* interview, of the following, the BEST way to assist the child would be to

   A. convince the child of his ability to be brave and grown-up
   B. play a competitive game with the child and let him win
   C. help the child express his fears and reassure him in accordance with reality
   D. tell the child that his problems are not so great as they may seem

9. Assume that one of your clients has many medical and social problems and needs a good deal of supportive case work help.
   Which one of the following approaches would generally be MOST appropriate for you to use in order to help this client cope with these problems?

   A. *Try* to make the client feel that his problems and situation are unique
   B. *Encourage* the client to be realistic about his situation and assure him that you understand and will do everything possible to help him cope
   C. *Emphasize* to the client those areas you feel you can work on and those which you can do nothing about
   D. *Urge* the client to refrain from taking action on serious matters without asking for your help first

10. Assume that, when you discuss with one of your elderly clients the advisability of applying to the department of socital services for financial assistance, the client becomes extremely upset about the prospect of having to be interviewed by "another stranger."
    Of the following, the BEST way to handle this situation would be to

    A. explain that applying for financial assistance is something the client must do by herself and for herself
    B. offer to accompany the client to social services if necessary, and work with the client toward greater future independence
    C. withdraw your suggestion, since the client's emotional health is your primary consideration
    D. suggest that the client take a personal friend to the interview to help with difficult questions, if necessary

11. Assume that a newspaper reporter calls and questions you regarding the long wait for treatment in the Emergency Room. Of the following, your *MOST* appropriate response would be to

    A. advise the reporter that the long wait is caused by an enormous increase in emergency cases
    B. refer the reporter to the director of social work
    C. tell the reporter that your hospital's emergency room is one of the most efficient in the city
    D. refer the reporter to the hospital employee responsible for public relations

12. When a worker interviews a patient whose problem seems to be typical of that of many other patients she has seen, of the following, it would be *MOST* appropriate to

    A. *attempt* to learn more about the individual circumstances of this patient's situation
    B. *handle* this case the same way as the others were handled
    C. *ask* another worker how she generally handles this type of problem
    D. *reassure* the patient by telling him that many other patients have similar problems

13. A patient without friends or relatives is being discharged from the hospital. He complains to you that his shoes are missing.
    Of the following, your *MOST* appropriate response would be to

    A. advise the patient that this is not a professional concern of yours and suggest that he speak to the ward nurse
    B. advise the patient that he will have to buy a pair of shoes from a nearby shoe store
    C. obtain a pair of shoes for the patient in the hospital clothing room
    D. tell the patient that he probably was not wearing shoes at the time he was admitted

14. The parents of a hospitalized child complain to you that their child is not getting proper nursing care. You have ample opportunity to observe what is happening on the pediatric ward and know that the nurses are extremely conscientious in caring for the children. Your *initial* interpretation of this complaint should be that, probably, the parents

    A. are projecting their anxiety about the child's health by criticizing the nurses
    B. are chronic complainers and must be treated accordingly
    C. may actually want to transfer the child to a more conveniently located hospital
    D. are trying to get special treatment for their child from the nurses

15. You are interviewing an unmarried, attractive young female patient who was in an automobile accident and will not be able to walk again. She says to you: "I'll never find a husband now that I'm crippled."
    In order to help her express her feelings freely, of the following, your *MOST* appropriate response would be:

    A. "You feel that no one will marry you because you can't walk."
    B. "Don't be silly. You have your whole life ahead of you."
    C. "That's not necessarily true. You're young and pretty and smart."
    D. "That may be true, but at least you're alive."

16. Assume that you are in your office completing some paperwork. A man enters and introduces himself as a close friend of one of your patients in the terminal cancer ward. He then asks if he can speak with you, and sits down in the chair next to your desk.
    Of the following, it would be MOST appropriate for you to say FIRST:

    A. "You probably want to know how your friend is coping with his condition."
    B. "You realize, of course, that your friend is dying of cancer."
    C. "What would you like to see me about?"
    D. "What problem would you like to discuss?"

17. During an interview with a new patient your mind wanders momentarily, and you have missed some details in the patient's story.
    Which one of the following would be most appropriate to say FIRST, before the patient continues?

    A. "And then what happened?" – so that the patient will think that you were paying attention all along.
    B. "Could you rephrase that?" – so that the patient will restate the details without being aware of your inattentiveness.
    C. "I'm sorry, I didn't get that, could you repeat that part?" – so that the patient will perceive you as an honest person.
    D. "Please continue". – so that the patient will not have to repeat something that was probably unimportant anyway.

18. Assume that one of your clients is telling you about her family situation. All of a sudden, she says: "Two of my kids go to school, and the third, who is seventeen, ..."
    Then she stops speaking.
    In this situation, of the following, it would be most appropriate for you to FIRST

    A. *state:* "works?"
    B. *state:* "quit school?"
    C. *ask:* "What about the third child?"
    D. *remain silent* for a few seconds

19. You have just started to interview a new client. He begins by telling you that he has been unemployed for the past three years and is receiving almost as much from welfare as he did when he was working. He continues talking along these lines, and then asks you why anybody would want to work when they can be on the dole and maintain almost the same standard of living.
    Of the following, your MOST appropriate response would be:

    A. "I don't personally approve of living in that manner."
    B. "It all depends on a person's values and standards."
    C. "If you are happy living like that, it's all right with me."
    D. "Let's not discuss that. Let's talk about your medical problems first."

20. During your second interview with a young woman, she asks you to drop all this professional stuff and just be friends.
 Which one of the following would be your appropriate response?

 A. "If we were friends, I would probably not be so effective in helping you deal with your problem."
 B. "That's O.K. with me, but you would have to be reassigned to a different worker."
 C. "That would be impossible under the rules and regulations of our agency."
 D. "I really don't think that's appropriate, and I'm a very busy person."

KEY (CORRECT ANSWERS)

1.	C	11.	D
2.	B	12.	A
3.	D	13.	C
4.	C	14.	A
5.	A	15.	A
6.	B	16.	C
7.	C	17.	C
8.	C	18.	D
9.	B	19.	B
10.	B	20.	A

TEST 2

DIRECTIONS: Each question or incomplete statement is followed by several suggested answers or completions, Select the one that *BEST* answers the question or completes the statement. *PRINT THE LETTER OF THE CORRECT ANSWER IN THE SPACE AT THE RIGHT.*

1. You are interviewing a young man who confides, in you that he is now on probation. In order to help this patient, you decide that it would be desirable to contact his probation officer to obtain additional information.
   Of the following, the BEST way to contact the probation officer would be

   A. *after* the interview, with the patient's consent
   B. *after* the interview, without the patient's consent
   C. *after* the interview, without telling the patient
   D. *during* the interview, with the patient present

2. You introduce yourself to a newly-hospitalized patient and offer to be of assistance if possible. The patient nods that she understands, and begins to discuss her 12-year-old daughter's truancy from school.
   Which one of the following responses would be most appropriate for you to make FIRST?

   A. *I understand your daughter's problem, but can we discuss your problems now?*
   B. *How do you feel this will affect you while you are in the hospital?*
   C. *Did your daughter fail any of her subjects because of her truancy?*
   D. *I have a very large caseload today. Perhaps we can discuss your daughter another time.*

3. You have been interviewing a patient for almost an hour and it is time for your next appointment. As you are about to finish, the patient begins to discuss a new problem.
   In this situation, it would generally be advisable to

   A. close the interview and make another appointment with the patient to discuss this problem
   B. allow the patient to *get things off his chest* before closing the interview
   C. ask the patient why he brought this problem up at the last moment
   D. tell the patient that you cannot discuss this problem because you will be late for your next appointment

4. Assume that you are completing a case involving a deteriorating relationship between the parents of a child who was hospitalized due to an accident caused by the child's father. Since counselling began upon admission of the child, there has been a marked improvement in the relationship between the parents and, in particular, between the child and the father. The child is about to be discharged from the hospital, and you are having an interview with the parents.
   Of the following, according to accepted casework practice, it would be *MOST* appropriate for you to

   A. assure the parents that, as a result of counselling, they are now *ideal* parents
   B. offer a continuation of counselling until the family's adjustment is stable
   C. review with the parents the *do's and don'ts* of being *good* parents
   D. explain to the parents how you helped them solve their problems

5. Assume that one of your clients, an adult male out-patient who has been coming to see you weekly for four months, fails to keep two appointments. The physician informs you that one of this patient's laboratory tests is positive, indicating the urgent need for follow-up medical care. You have sent the patient a telegram, but he has not replied after a reasonable length of time.
   According to accepted casework practice, of the following, the MOST advisable action for you to take would be to

   A. *contact* a neighbor of the patient and ask the neighbor to persuade the patient to return to the hospital
   B. *inform* a member of the patient's family of the positive; test result and emphasize the urgency of the situation
   C. *write* to the patient and explain the dangers of not returning to the hospital for treatment
   D. *make* an emergency visit to the patient at home and tell him about the positive test result and the importance of returning to the hospital

6. Assume that you are trying to establish the identity of an elderly woman who was brought to the Emergency Room by the police, who found her on the street, somewhat disoriented. The doctor decides to admit the woman, whose blood pressure is elevated, and who has an open ulcerated wound on her leg. She is very talkative about events long in the past, can't recall where she lives, but keeps speaking of having to *go home to give her sister breakfast*. The police have found that she has a card giving her name and an address which is three blocks from the hospital, but the telephone company has no listing for her.
   Of the following, your MOST advisable action would be to

   A. ask the hospital security guards to make a visit to the address on the card and tell any relatives of the woman that she is hospitalized
   B. have a visiting nurse make a visit to the address and check on the sister's possible need for food and medical attention
   C. call the social service exchange to determine whether the woman is known to any agency and what information they may have about her and her sister
   D. make a visit to the address on the card in order to obtai more information about the woman

7. You are a worker assigned to the alcoholism clinic. One of your clients appears for an interview in an intoxicated condition. Of the following, your MOST appropriate action would be to

   A. discuss the patient's drinking problem with him in no uncertain terms
   B. make another appointment and point out to the patient that he cannot be interviewed while intoxicated
   C. threaten to close the case and discharge the patient if he does not sober up
   D. recommend psychological testing to determine why the patient persists in drinking in spite of counselling

8. As a worker in the family planning clinic, you are counselling an 18-year-old unmarried patient who is pregnant. She is in a state of conflict, because she wants an abortion, but her boyfriend is encouraging her to marry him and bear the child.
Of the following, your MOST appropriate action would be to

    A. ask the patient why she was careless after receiving guidance from the family planning clinic
    B. encourage the patient to make the decision for herself, and Be supportive of her choice
    C. stress the positive qualities of her boyfriend, who is offering to marry her
    D. determine whether the conflict may derive from the patient's religious upbringing

9. Assume that one of your cases, a woman who has given birth three days ago, is now verbally abusive to the staff, and refuses to see her infant. Of the following, your MOST appropriate course of action would be to

    A. scold the woman for her childish behavior
    B. attempt to convince the woman that once she sees the baby she will feel much better
    C. speak with the woman in an effort to understand her behavior
    D. tell the woman that she will be transferred to the psychiatric unit if she does not behave

10. Assume that you are interviewing an unmarried female patient in the Emergency Room. The doctor has just told her that she must be admitted to the hospital on an emergency basis, but she refuses to accept this recommendation because she has three small children, has no one to care for them, and does not want to leave them alone.
Of the following, the most appropriate action for you to take FIRST would be to

    A. suggest that the patient try to enlist neighbors to help look after the children
    B. ask the doctor to admit the children with their mother on an emergency basis
    C. try to locate the children's father and ask him to look after the children
    D. explain to the patient that it is possible for you to arrange for care of the children

11. Assume that you are assigned to the methadone maintenance clinic. As you are about to finish an interview, your client asks you to lend him ten dollars. Of the following, your most appropriate FIRST action would be to

    A. inform the client that it is against hospital policy for a worker to lend money to a patient
    B. lend the client the ten dollars
    C. suggest that the client borrow the money from a personal friend
    D. advise the client to apply to the department of social services for an emergency grant

12. You are interviewing a young unmarried woman who is pregnant, says that she is not sure she can care for her baby properly, and is considering requesting an abortion. Of the following, your MOST appropriate response would be:

    A. *What do you think of as proper care for your baby?*
    B. *I'm sure you will be an excellent mother.*
    C. *Do you know who the father is?*
    D. *How long have you been pregnant?*

13. You are interviewing a married patient with two young children with regard to her impending surgery. Suddenly, she asks if you are married. Of the following, the MOST appropriate response would be to tell her

    A. whether you are married, and then ask why she wants to know
    B. you are not now married, but that you are engaged to be married
    C. this is irrelevant, and continue discussing her situation
    D. you used to be married, but that you are now divorced

14. You are visiting a new patient on your assigned ward. After introducing yourself and offering to be of assistance, the patient begins to tell you a lengthy story relating to her illness. According to accepted interviewing techniques, of the following, it would be MOST appropriate for you to indicate your concern and interest by

    A. briefly commenting or asking questions, indicating that you are grasping the essential points
    B. saying nothing, so as not to interrupt the patient's train of thought
    C. interrupting frequently to clarify points you do not fully comprehend
    D. asking the patient to pause at periodic intervals so that you may proceed to ask structured questions

15. You have been counseling an adult patient on the cancer ward on a weekly basis for about a month and it is now time to decide where the patient will live after being discharged from the hospital.
    According to accepted practice, the FINAL decision on this matter should be made by

    A. you, the case worker
    B. the patient's relatives
    C. the patient, with the case worker's help
    D. the patient and the doctors

16. Assume that a patient in your caseload asks you for specific advice regarding his unhappy marital situation. In deciding whether to respond to this request, you should generally consider all of the following EXCEPT

    A. any possible underlying anxiety the patient may have
    B. the patient's ability to carry out the advice
    C. the seriousness of the patient's situation
    D. whether the client will accept or reject your advice

17. According to accepted casework practice, when interviewing a young child it is considered especially important for the worker to closely observe the child's behavior, feelings, and mood, in addition to listening to what the child says, MAINLY because such observation should

    A. provide significant diagnostic information about the child
    B. help the child feel closer to the worker
    C. enable the worker to sense the right time to console the child
    D. give the worker clues as to when to humor the child

18. You find it necessary to refer a client for psychiatric help upon discharge. The client consents to this plan, but asks you to omit from your report certain information he has told you in confidence. You feel that the psychiatrist's knowledge of this information would be of great benefit in helping your client.
For you to go ahead and include this information in your report to the psychiatrist, without the client's consent, would be considered

    A. *good practice*, because the psychiatrist will need all available information about the client
    B. *bad practice*, because this action would be a breach of confidence
    C. *good practice*, because helping the client is the primary goal of case work
    D. *bad practice,* because the patient would probably find out eventually that this information was disclosed

19. You are interviewing a woman who has suffered a severe beating from her husband, is obviously upset, and embarrassed about having to relate the details to you.
Of the following, the MOST appropriate way for you to handle this situation would be to

    A. insist that she tell you the whole story, including the details
    B. postpone discussion of the beating until the woman feels better
    C. tell the woman to omit the details for now, and ask her how you can be of help
    D. postpone this interview until the husband is available to present his side of the story

20. You are making discharge plans for an alert, 78-year-old retired school teacher who is recovering satisfactorily from a minor operation. One day, when you come to her room, she fails to recognize you and tells you disconnected stories about people she knew in childhood.
Of the following, the MOST appropriate way to handle this changed situation would be to

    A. tell the patient she had better *snap out of it*
    B. advise the patient that you will return when she starts talking sense
    C. confer with the attending physician about this change in the patient's condition
    D. suggest to the physician that the discharge plan be changed to recommend admission to a State hospital

KEY (CORRECT ANSWERS)

1.	A	11.	A
2.	B	12.	A
3.	A	13.	A
4.	B	14.	A
5.	D	15.	C
6.	D	16.	D
7.	B	17.	A
8.	B	18.	B
9.	C	19.	C
10.	D	20.	C

EXAMINATION SECTION
TEST 1

DIRECTIONS: Each question or incomplete statement is followed by several suggested answers or completions. Select the one that BEST answers the question or completes the statement. *PRINT THE LETTER OF THE CORRECT ANSWER IN THE SPACE AT THE RIGHT.*

1. Deviant behavior is a sociological term used to describe behavior which is not in accord with generally accepted standards. This may include juvenile delinquency, adult criminality, mental or physical illness.
   Comparison of normal with deviant behavior is useful to social workers because it

   A. makes it possible to establish watertight behavioral descriptions
   B. provides evidence of differential social behavior which distinguishes deviant from normal behavior
   C. indicates that deviant behavior is of no concern to social workers
   D. provides no evidence that social role is a determinant of behavior

2. Alcoholism may affect an individual client's ability to function as a spouse, parent, worker, and citizen.
   A social worker's MAIN responsibility to a client with a history of alcoholism is to

   A. interpret to the client the causes of alcoholism as a disease syndrome
   B. work with the alcoholic's family to accept him as he is and stop trying to reform him
   C. encourage the family of the alcoholic to accept casework treatment
   D. determine the origins of his particular drinking problem, establish a diagnosis, and work out a treatment plan for him

3. There is a trend to regard narcotic addiction as a form of illness for which the current methods of intervention have not been effective.
   Research on the combination of social, psychological, and physical causes of addiction would indicate that social workers should

   A. oppose hospitalization of addicts in institutions
   B. encourage the addict to live normally at home
   C. recognize that there is no successful treatment for addiction and act accordingly
   D. use the existing community facilities differentially for each addict

4. A study of social relationships among delinquent and non-delinquent youth has shown that

   A. delinquent youth generally conceal their true feelings and maintain furtive social contacts
   B. delinquents are more impulsive and vivacious than law-abiding boys
   C. non-delinquent youths diminish their active social relationships in order to sublimate any anti-social impulses
   D. delinquent and non-delinquent youths exhibit similar characteristics of impulsiveness and vivaciousness

5. The one of the following which is the CHIEF danger of interpreting the delinquent behavior of a child in terms of morality *alone* when attempting to get at its causes is that

   A. this tends to overlook the likelihood that the causes of the child's actions are more than a negation of morality and involve varied symptoms of disturbance
   B. a child's moral outlook toward life and society is largely colored by that of his parents, thus encouraging parent-child conflict
   C. too careful a consideration of the moral aspects of the offense and of the child's needs may often negate the demands of justice in a case
   D. standards of morality may be of no concern to the delinquent and he may not realize the seriousness of his offenses

6. Experts in the field of personnel administration are generally agreed that an employee should not be under the immediate supervision of more than one supervisor. A certain worker, because of an emergency situation, divides his time equally between two limited caseloads on a prearranged time schedule. Each unit has a different supervisor, and the worker performs substantially the same duties in each caseload.
The above statement is pertinent in this situation CHIEFLY because

   A. each supervisor, feeling that the cases in her unit should have priority, may demand too much of the worker's time
   B. the two supervisors may have different standards of work performance and may prefer different methods of doing the work
   C. the worker works part-time on each caseload and may not have full knowledge or control of the situation in either caseload
   D. the task of evaluating the worker's services will be doubled, with two supervisors instead of one having to rate his work

7. Experts in modern personnel management generally agree that employees on all job levels should be permitted to offer suggestions for improving work methods.
Of the following, the CHIEF limitation of such suggestions is that they may, at times,

   A. be offered primarily for financial reward and not show genuine interest in improvement of work methods
   B. be directed towards making individual jobs easier
   C. be restricted by the employees' fear of radically changing the work methods favored by their supervisors
   D. show little awareness of the effects on the overall objectives and functions of the entire agency

8. Through the supervisory process and relationship, the supervisor is trying to help workers gain increased self-awareness.
Of the following statements concerning this process, the one which is MOST accurate is:

   A. Self-awareness is developed gradually so that worker can learn to control his own reactions.
   B. Worker is expected to be introspective primarily for his own enlightenment.
   C. Supervisor is trying to help worker handle any emotional difficulties he may reveal.
   D. Worker is expected at the onset to share and determine with the supervisor what in his previous background makes it difficult for him to use certain ideas.

9. The one of the following statements concerning principles in the learning process which is LEAST accurate is:

   A. Some degree of regression on the part of the worker is usually natural in the process of development and this should be accepted by the supervisor.
   B. When a beginning worker shows problems, the supervisor should first handle this behavior as a personality difficulty.
   C. It has been found in the work training process that some degree of resistance is usually inevitable.
   D. The emotional content of work practice may tend to set up *blind spots* in workers.

10. Of the following, the one that represents the BEST basis for planning the content of a successful staff development program is the

   A. time available for meetings
   B. chief social problems of the community
   C. common needs of the staff workers as related to the situations with which they are dealing
   D. experimental programs conducted by other agencies

11. In planning staff development seminars, the MOST valuable topics for discussion are likely to be those selected from

   A. staff suggestions based on the staff's interest and needs
   B. topics recommended for consideration by professional organizations
   C. topics selected by the administration based on demonstrated limitations of staff skill and knowledge
   D. topics selected by the administration based on a combination of staff interest and objectivity evaluated staff needs

12. Staff meetings designed to promote professional staff development are MOST likely to achieve this goal when

   A. there is the widest participation among all staff members who attend the meetings
   B. participation by the most skilled and experienced staff members is predominant
   C. participation by selected staff members is planned before the meeting sessions
   D. supervisory personnel take major responsibility for participation

13. Assume that you are the leader of a conference attended by representatives of various city and private agencies. After the conference has been underway for a considerable time, you realize that the representative of one of these agencies has said nothing. It would generally be BEST for you to

   A. ask him if he would like to say anything
   B. ask the group a pertinent question that he would probably be best able to answer
   C. make no special effort to include him in the conversation
   D. address the next question you planned to ask to him directly

14. A member of a decision-making conference generally makes his BEST contribution to the conference when he

   A. compromises on his own point of view and accepts most of the points of other conference members
   B. persuades the conference to accept all or most of his points

C. persuades the conference to accept his major proposals but will yield on the minor ones
D. succeeds in integrating his ideas with the ideas of the other conference members

15. Of the following, the LEAST accurate statement concerning the compilation and use of statistics in administration is:

    A. Interpretation of statistics is as necessary as their compilation.
    B. Statistical records of expenditures and services are one of the bases for budget preparation.
    C. Statistics on the quality of services rendered to the community will clearly delineate the human values achieved.
    D. The results achieved from collecting and compiling statistics must be in keeping with the cost and effort required.

16. An important administrative problem is how precisely to define the limits on authority that is delegated to subordinate supervisors.
    Such definition of limits of authority SHOULD be

    A. as precise as possible and practicable in all areas
    B. as precise as possible and practicable in all areas of function, but should allow considerable flexibility in the area of personnel management
    C. as precise as possible and practicable in the area of personnel management, but should allow considerable flexibility in the areas of function
    D. in general terms so as to allow considerable flexibility both in the areas of function and in the areas of personnel management

17. The LEAST important of the following reasons why a particular activity should be assigned to a unit which performs activities dissimilar to it is that

    A. close coordination is needed between the particular activity and other activities performed by the unit
    B. it will enhance the reputation and prestige of the unit supervisor
    C. the unit makes frequent use of the results of this particular activity
    D. the unit supervisor has a sound knowledge and understanding of the particular activity

18. The MOST important of the following reasons why the average resident of a deteriorated slum neighborhood resists relocation to an area in the suburbs with better physical accommodations is that he

    A. does not recognize as undesirable the characteristics which are responsible for deterioration of the neighborhood
    B. has some expectation of neighborly assistance in his old home in times of stress and adversity
    C. hopes for better days when he may be able to become a figure of some importance and envy in the old neighborhood
    D. is attuned to the noise of the city and fears the quiet of the suburb

19. From a psychological and sociological point of view, the MOST important of the following dangers to the persons living in an economically depressed area in which the only step taken by governmental and private social agencies to assist these persons is the granting of a dole is that

    A. industry will be reluctant to expand its operations in that area
    B. the dole will encourage additional non-producers to enter the area
    C. the residents of the area will probably have to find their own solution to their problems
    D. their permanent dependency will be fostered

20. The term *real wages* is GENERALLY used by economists to mean the

    A. amount of take-home pay left after taxes, social security, and other such deductions have been made by the employer
    B. average wage actually earned during a calendar or fiscal year
    C. family income expressed on a per capita basis
    D. wages expressed in terms of its buyer power

21. It has, at times, been suggested that an effective way to eradicate juvenile delinquency would be to arrest and punish the parents for the criminal actions of their delinquent children.
    The one of the following which is the CHIEF defect of this proposal is that

    A. it fails to get at the cause of the delinquent act and tends to further weaken disturbed parent-child relationships
    B. since the criminally inclined child has apparently demonstrated little love or affection for his parent, the child will be unlikely to amend his behavior in order to avoid hurting his parent
    C. the child who commits anti-social acts does so in many cases in order to hurt his parents so that this proposal would not only increase the parents' sorrow, but would also serve as an incentive to more delinquency by the child
    D. the punishment should be limited to the person who commits the illegal action rather than to those who are most interested in his welfare

22. Surveys which have compared the relative stability of marriages between white persons with marriages between non-white persons in this country have shown that, among Blacks, there is

    A. a significantly higher percentage of spouses absent from the household than among whites
    B. a significantly higher percentage of spouses absent from the household than among whites living in the South, but the opposite is true in the Northeast
    C. a significantly lower percentage of spouses absent from the household than among whites
    D. no significant difference in the percentage of spouses absent from the household when compared with the white population

23. A phenomenon found in the cultural and recreational patterns of European immigrant families in America is that, generally, the foreign-born adults

   A. as well as their children, tend soon to forget their old-world activities and adopt the cultural and recreational customs of America
   B. as well as their children, tend to retain and continue their old-world cultural and recreational pursuits, and find it equally difficult to adopt those of America
   C. tend soon to drop their old pursuits and adopt the cultural and recreational patterns of America while their children find it somewhat more difficult to make this change
   D. tend to retain and continue their old-world cultural and recreational pursuits while their children tend to rapidly replace these by the games and cultural patterns of America

23.____

24. Certain mores of migrant groups are strengthened under the impact of their contact with the native society while other mores are weakened.
In the case of Puerto Ricans who have come to the city, the effect of such contact upon their traditional family structure has been a

   A. strengthening of the former maternalistic family structure
   B. strengthening of the former paternalistic family structure
   C. weakening of the former maternalistic family structure
   D. weakening of the former paternalistic family structure

24.____

25. Administrative reviews and special studies of independent experts, as reported by the Department of Health, Education and Welfare, indicate that the proportion of recipients of public assistance who receive such assistance through *wilful misrepresentation* of the facts is

   A. less than 1% B. about 4%
   C. between 4% and 7% D. between 7% and 10%

25.____

KEY (CORRECT ANSWERS)

1.	B	11.	D
2.	D	12.	A
3.	D	13.	B
4.	B	14.	D
5.	A	15.	C
6.	B	16.	A
7.	D	17.	B
8.	A	18.	B
9.	B	19.	D
10.	C	20.	D

21. A
22. A
23. D
24. D
25. A

TEST 2

DIRECTIONS: Each question or incomplete statement is followed by several suggested answers or completions. Select the one that BEST answers the question or completes the statement. *PRINT THE LETTER OF THE CORRECT ANSWER IN THE SPACE AT THE RIGHT.*

1. In order to meet more adequately the public assistance needs occasioned by sudden changes in the national economy, social service agencies, in general, recommend, as a matter of preference, that

    A. each locality build up reserve funds to care for needy unemployed persons in order to avoid a breakdown of local resources such as occurred during the depression
    B. the federal government assume total responsibility for the administration of public assistance
    C. state settlement laws be strictly enforced so that unemployed workers will be encouraged to move from the emergency industry centers to their former homes
    D. a federal-state-local program of general assistance be established with need as the only eligibility requirement
    E. eligibility requirements be tightened to assure that only legitimately worthy local residents receive the available assistance

1.____

2. The MOST practical method of maintaining income for the majority of aged persons who are no longer able to work, or for the families of those workers who are deceased, is a(n)

    A. comprehensive system of non-categorical assistance on a basis of cash payments
    B. integrated system of public assistance and extensive work relief programs
    C. co-ordinated system of providing care in institutions and foster homes
    D. system of contributory insurance in which a cash benefit is paid as a matter of right
    E. expanded system of diagnostic and treatment centers

2.____

3. With the establishment of insurance and assistance programs under the Social Security Act, many institutional programs for the aged have tended to the greatest extent toward an increased emphasis on providing, of the following types of assistance,

    A. care for the aged by denominational groups
    B. care for children requiring institutional treatment
    C. recreational facilities for the able-bodied aged
    D. training facilities in industrial homework for the aged
    E. care for the chronically ill and infirm aged

3.____

4. Of the following terms, the one which BEST describes the Social Security Act is

    A. enabling legislation
    B. regulatory statute
    C. appropriations act
    D. act of mandamus
    E. provisional enactment

4.____

5. Of the following, the term which MOST accurately describes an appropriation is

   A. authority to spend
   B. itemized estimate
   C. *fund* accounting
   D. anticipated expenditure
   E. executive budget

6. When business expansion causes a demand for labor, the worker group which benefits MOST immediately is the group comprising

   A. employed workers
   B. inexperienced workers under 21 years of age
   C. experienced workers 21 to 25 years of age
   D. inexperienced older workers
   E. experienced workers over 40 years of age

7. The MOST important failure in our present system of providing social work services in local communities is the

   A. absence of adequate facilities for treating mental illness
   B. lack of coordination of available data and service in the community
   C. poor quality of the casework services provided by the public agencies
   D. limitations of the probation and parole services
   E. inadequacy of private family welfare services

8. Recent studies of the relationship between incidence of illness and the use of available treatment services among various population groups in the United States show that

   A. while lower-income families use medical services with greater frequency, total expenditures are greater among the upper-income groups
   B. although the average duration of a period of medical care increases with increasing income, the average frequency of obtaining care decreases with increasing income
   C. adequacy of medical service is inversely related to frequency of illness and size of family income
   D. families in the higher-income brackets have a heavier incidence of illness and make greater use of medical services than do those in the lower-income brackets
   E. both as to frequency and duration, the distribution of illness falls equally on all groups, but the use of medical services increases with income

9. The category of disease which most public health departments and authorities usually are NOT equipped to handle *directly* is that of

   A. chronic disease
   B. bronchial disturbances
   C. venereal disease
   D. mosquito-borne diseases
   E. incipient forms of tuberculosis

10. Recent statistical analyses of the causes of death in the United States indicate that medical science has now reached the stage where it would be preferable to increase its research toward control, among the following, PRINCIPALLY of

    A. accidents
    B. suicides
    C. communicable disease
    D. chronic disease
    E. infant mortality

11. Although the distinction between mental disease and mental deficiency is fairly definite, both these conditions USUALLY represent

    A. diseases of one part or organ of the body rather than of the whole person
    B. an inadequacy existing from birth or shortly afterwards and appearing as a simplicity of intelligence
    C. a deficiency developing later in life and characterized by distortions of attitude and belief
    D. inadequacies in meeting life situations and in conducting one's affairs
    E. somewhat transitory conditions characterized by disturbances of consciousness

12. According to studies made by reliable medical research organizations in the United States, differences among the states in proportion of physicians to population are MOST directly related to the

    A. geographic resources among the states
    B. skill of the physicians
    C. relative proportions of urban and rural people in the population of the states
    D. number of specialists in the ranks of the physicians
    E. health status of the people in the various states

13. One of the MAIN advantages of incorporating a charitable organization is that

    A. gifts or property of a corporation cannot be held in perpetuity
    B. gifts to unincorporated charitable organizations are not deductible from the taxable income
    C. incorporation gives less legal standing or *personality* than an informal partnership
    D. members of a corporation cannot be held liable for debts contracted by the organization
    E. a corporate organization cannot be sued

14. The BASIC principle underlying a social security program is that the government should provide

    A. aid to families that is not dependent on state or local participation
    B. assistance to any worthy family unable to maintain itself independently
    C. protection to individuals against some of the social risks that are inherent in an industrialized society
    D. safeguards against those factors leading to economic depression

15. The activities of state and local public welfare agencies are dependent to a large degree on the public assistance program of the federal government.
    The one of the following which the federal government has NOT been successful in achieving within the local agencies is the

    A. broadening of the scope of public assistance administration
    B. expansion of the categorical programs
    C. improvement of the quality of service given to clients
    D. standardization of the administration of general assistance programs

16. Of the following statements, the one which BEST describes the federal government's position, as stated in the Social Security Act, with regard to tests of character or fitness to be administered by local or state welfare departments to prospective clients is that

    A. no tests of character are required but they are not specifically prohibited
    B. if tests of character are used, they must be uniform throughout the state
    C. tests of character are contrary to the philosophy of the federal government and are to be considered illegal
    D. no tests of character are required, and assistance to those states that use them will be withheld

17. An increase in the size of the welfare grant may increase the cost of the welfare program not only in terms of those already on the welfare rolls, but because it may result in an increase in the number of people on the rolls.
    The CHIEF reason that an increase in the size of the grant may cause an increase in the number of people on the rolls is that the increased grant may

    A. induce low-salaried wage earners to apply for assistance rather than continue at their menial jobs
    B. make eligible for assistance many people whose resources are just above the previous standard
    C. induce many people to apply for assistance who hesitated to do so because of meagerness of the previous grant
    D. make relatives less willing to contribute because the welfare grant can more adequately cover their dependents' needs

18. One of the MAIN differences between the use of casework methods by a public welfare agency and by a private welfare agency is that the public welfare agency

    A. requires that the applicant be eligible for the services it offers
    B. cannot maintain a non-judgmental attitude toward its clients because of legal requirements
    C. places less emphasis on efforts to change the behavior of its clients
    D. must be more objective in its approach to the client because public funds are involved

19. All definitions of social casework include certain major assumptions.
    Of the following, the one which is NOT considered a major assumption is that

    A. the individual and society are interdependent
    B. social forces influence behavior and attitudes, affording opportunity for self-development and contribution to the world in which we live
    C. reconstruction of the total personality and reorganization of the total environment are specific goals
    D. the client is a responsible participant at every step in the solution of his problems

20. In order to provide those services to problem families which will help restore them to a self-maintaining status, it is necessary to FIRST

    A. develop specific plans to meet the individual needs of the problem family
    B. reduce the size of those caseloads composed of multi-problem families
    C. remove them from their environment and provide them with the means of overcoming their dependency
    D. identify the factors causing their dependency and creating problems for them

21. Of the following, the type of service which can provide the client with the MOST enduring help is that service which

    A. provides him with material aid and relieves the stress of his personal problems
    B. assists him to do as much as he can for himself and leaves him free to make his own decisions
    C. directs his efforts towards returning to a self-maintaining status and provides him with desirable goals
    D. gives him the feeling that the agency is interested in him as an individual and stands ready to assist him with his problems

22. Psychiatric interpretation of unconscious motivations can bring childhood conflicts into the framework of adult understanding and open the way for them to be resolved, but the interpretation must come from within the client.
    This statement means MOST NEARLY that

    A. treatment is merely diagnosis in reverse
    B. explaining a client to himself will lead to the resolution of his problems
    C. the client must arrive at an understanding of his problems
    D. unresolved childhood conflicts create problems for the adult

23. A significant factor in the United States economic picture is the state of the labor market. Of the following, the MOST important development affecting the labor market has been

    A. an expansion of the national defense effort creating new plant capacity
    B. the general increase in personal income as a result of an increase in overtime pay in manufacturing industries
    C. the growth of manufacturing as a result of automation
    D. a demand for a large number of jobs resulting from new job applicants as well as from displacement of workers by automation

24. A typical characteristic of the United States population over 65 is that MOST of them

    A. are independent and capable of self-support
    B. live in their own homes but require various supportive services
    C. live in institutions for the aged
    D. require constant medical attention at home or in an institution

25. The one of the following factors which is MOST important in preventing persons 65 years of age and older from getting employment is the

    A. misconceptions by employers of skills and abilities of senior citizens
    B. lack of skill in modern industrial techniques of persons in this age group
    C. social security laws restricting employment of persons in this age group
    D. unwillingness of persons in this age group to continue supporting themselves

KEY (CORRECT ANSWERS)

1. D
2. D
3. E
4. A
5. A

6. B
7. B
8. C
9. A
10. D

11. D
12. C
13. D
14. C
15. D

16. A
17. B
18. C
19. C
20. D

21. B
22. C
23. D
24. B
25. A

EXAMINATION SECTION
TEST 1

DIRECTIONS: Each question or incomplete statement is followed by several suggested answers or completions. Select the one that BEST answers the question or completes the statement. *PRINT THE LETTER OF THE CORRECT ANSWER IN THE SPACE AT THE RIGHT.*

1. An interview is BEST conducted in private primarily because
    A. the person interviewed will tend to be less self-conscious
    B. the interviewer will be able to maintain his continuity of thought better
    C. it will insure that the interview is "off the record"
    D. people tend to "show off" before an audience

2. An interviewer can BEST establish a good relationship with the person being interviewed by
    A. assuming casual interest in the statements made by the person being interviewed
    B. taking the point of view of the person interviewed
    C. controlling the interview to a major extent
    D. showing a genuine interest in the person

3. An interviewer will be better able to understand the person interviewed and his problems if he recognizes that much of the person's behavior is due to motives
    A. which are deliberate
    B. of which he is unaware
    C. which are inexplicable
    D. which are kept under control

4. An interviewer's attention must be directed toward himself as well as toward the person interviewed.
   This statement means that the interviewer should
    A. keep in mind the extent to which his own prejudices may influence his judgment
    B. rationalize the statements made by the person interviewed
    C. gain the respect and confidence of the person interviewed
    D. avoid being too impersonal

5. More complete expression will be obtained from a person being interviewed if the interviewer can create the impression that
    A. the data secured will become part of a permanent record
    B. official information must be accurate in every detail
    C. it is the duty of the person interviewed to give accurate data
    D. the person interviewed is participating in a discussion of his own problems

6. The practice of asking leading questions should be avoided in an interview because the
    A. interviewer risks revealing his attitudes to the person being interviewed
    B. interviewer may be led to ignore the objective attitudes of the person interviewed
    C. answers may be unwarrantedly influenced
    D. person interviewed will resent the attempt to lead him and will be less cooperative

6._____

7. A good technique for the interviewer to use in an effort to secure reliable data and to reduce the possibility of misunderstanding is to
    A. use casual undirected conversation, enabling the person being interviewed to talk about himself, and thus secure the desired information
    B. adopt the procedure of using direct questions regularly
    C. extract the desired information from the person being interviewed by putting him on the defensive
    D. explain to the person being interviewed the information desired and the reason for needing it

7._____

8. You are interviewing a patient to determine whether she is eligible for medical assistance. Of the many questions that you have to ask her, some are routine questions that patients tend to answer willingly and easily. Other questions are more personal and some patients tend to resent being asked them and avoid answering them directly.
   For you to begin the interview with the more personal questions would be
    A. *desirable*, because the end of the interview will go smoothly and the patient will be left with a warm feeling
    B. *undesirable*, because the patient might not know the answers to the questions
    C. *desirable*, because you will be able to return to these questions later to verify the accuracy of the responses
    D. *undesirable*, because you might antagonize the patient before you have had a chance to establish rapport

8._____

9. While interviewing a patient about her family composition, the patient asks you whether you are married.
   Of the following, the MOST appropriate way for you to handle this situation is to
    A. answer the question briefly and redirect her back to the topic under discussion
    B. refrain from answering the question and proceed with the interview
    C. advise the patient that it is more important that she answer your questions than that you answer hers, and proceed with the interview
    D. promise the patient that you will answer her question later, in the hope that she will forget, and redirect her back to the topic under discussion

9._____

10. In response to a question about his employment history, a patient you are interviewing rambles and talks about unrelated matters.
    Of the following, the MOST appropriate course of action for you to take FIRST is to

10._____

A. ask questions to direct the patient back to his employment history
B. advise him to concentrate on your questions and not to discuss irrelevant information
C. ask him why he is resisting a discussion of his employment history
D. advise him that if you cannot get the information you need, he will not be eligible for medical assistance

11. Suppose that a person you are interviewing becomes angry at some of the questions you have asked, calls you meddlesome and nosy, and states that she will not answer those questions.
    Of the following, which is the BEST action for you to take?
    A. Explain the reasons the questions are asked and the importance of the answers
    B. Inform the interviewee that you are only doing your job and advise her that she should answer your questions or leave the office
    C. Report to your supervisor what the interviewee called you and refuse to continue the interview
    D. End the interview and tell the interviewee she will not be serviced by your department

12. Suppose that during the course of an interview the interviewee demands in a very rude way that she be permitted to talk to your supervisor or someone in charge.
    Which of the following is probably the BEST way to handle this situation?
    A. Inform your supervisor of the demand and ask her to speak to the interviewee
    B. Pay no attention to the demands of the interviewee and continue the interview
    C. Report to your supervisor and tell her to get another interviewer for this interviewee
    D. Tell her you are the one "in charge" and that she should talk to you

13. Of the following, the outcome of an interview by an aide depends MOST heavily on the
    A. personality of the interviewee
    B. personality of the aide
    C. subject matter of the questions asked
    D. interaction between aide and interviewee

14. Some patients being interviewed are primarily interested in making a favorable impression.
    The aide should be aware of the fact that such patients are more likely than other patients to
    A. try to anticipate the answers the interviewer is looking for
    B. answer all questions openly and frankly
    C. try to assume the role of interviewer
    D. be anxious to get the interview over as quickly as possible

15. The type of interview which an aide usually conducts is substantially different from most interviewing situations in all of the following aspects EXCEPT the
    A. setting
    B. kinds of clients
    C. techniques employed
    D. kinds of problems

15.____

16. During an interview, an aide uses a "leading question."
    This type of question is so-called because it generally
    A. starts a series of questions about one topic
    B. suggests the answer which the aide wants
    C. forms the basis for a following "trick" question
    D. sets, at the beginning, the tone of the interview

16.____

17. Casework interviewing is always directed to the client and his situation.
    The one of the following which is the MOST accurate statement with respect to the proper focus of an interview is that the
    A. caseworker limits the client to concentration on objective data
    B. client is generally permitted to talk about facts and feelings with no direction from the caseworker
    C. main focus in casework interviews is on feelings rather than facts
    D. caseworker is responsible for helping the client focus on any material which seems to be related to his problems or difficulties

17.____

18. Assume that you are conducting a training program for the caseworkers under your supervision. At one of the sessions, you discuss the problem of interviewing a dull and stupid client who gives a slow and disconnected case history.
    The BEST of the following interviewing methods for you to recommend in such a case in order to ascertain facts is for the caseworker to
    A. ask the client leading questions requiring "yes" or "no" answers
    B. request the client to limit his narration to the essential facts so that the interview can be kept as brief as possible
    C. review the story with the client, patiently asking simple questions
    D. tell the client that unless he is more cooperative he cannot be helped to solve his problem

18.____

19. A recent development in casework interviewing procedure, known as multiple-client interviewing, consists of interviews of the entire family at the same time. However, this may not be an effective casework method in certain situations.
    Of the following, the situation in which the standard individual interview would be preferable is when
    A. family member derive consistent and major gratification from assisting each other in their destructive responses
    B. there is a crucial family conflict to which the members are reacting
    C. the family is overwhelmed by interpersonal anxieties which have not been explored
    D. the worker wants to determine the pattern of family interaction to further his diagnostic understanding

19.____

20. A follow-up interview was arranged for an applicant in order that he could furnish 20.____
certain requested evidence. At this follow-up interview, the applicant still fails
to furnish the necessary evidence.
It would be MOST advisable for you to
   A. advise the applicant that he is now considered ineligible
   B. ask the applicant how soon he can get the necessary evidence and set a
      date for another interview
   C. question the applicant carefully and thoroughly to determine if he has
      misrepresented or falsified any information
   D. set a date for another interview and tell the applicant to get the necessary
      evidence by that time

KEY (CORRECT ANSWERS)

1.	A	11.	A
2.	D	12.	A
3.	B	13.	D
4.	A	14.	A
5.	D	15.	C
6.	C	16.	B
7.	D	17.	D
8.	D	18.	C
9.	A	19.	A
10.	A	20.	B

TEST 2

DIRECTIONS: Each question or incomplete statement is followed by several suggested answers or completions. Select the one that BEST answers the question or completes the statement. *PRINT THE LETTER OF THE CORRECT ANSWER IN THE SPACE AT THE RIGHT.*

1. In interviewing, the practice of anticipating an applicant's answers to questions is generally
    A. *desirable*, because it is effective and economical when it is necessary to interview large numbers of applicants
    B. *desirable*, because many applicants have language difficulties
    C. *undesirable*, because it is the inalienable right of every person to answer as he sees fit
    D. *undesirable*, because applicants may tend to agree with the answer proposed by the interviewer even when the answer is not entirely correct

2. When an initial interview is being conducted, one way of starting is to explain the purpose of the interview to the applicant.
    The practice of starting the interview with such an explanation is generally
    A. *desirable*, because the applicant can then understand why the interview is necessary and what will be accomplished by it
    B. *desirable*, because it creates the rapport which is necessary to successful interviewing
    C. *undesirable*, because time will be saved by starting directly with the questions which must be asked
    D. *undesirable*, because the interviewer should have the choice of starting an interview in any manner he prefers

3. For you to use responses such as "That's interesting," "Uh-huh," and "Good" during an interview with a patient is
    A. *desirable*, because they indicate that the investigator is attentive
    B. *undesirable*, because they are meaningless to the patient
    C. *desirable*, because the investigator is not supposed to talk excessively
    D. *undesirable*, because they tend to encourage the patient to speak freely

4. During the course of a routine interview, the BEST tone of voice for an interviewer to use is
    A. authoritative   B. uncertain
    C. formal   D. conversational

5. It is recommended that interviews which inquire into the personal background of an individual should be held in private.
    The BEST reason for this practice is that privacy
    A. allows the individual to talk freely about the details of his background
    B. induces contemplative thought on the part of the interviewed individual
    C. prevents any interruptions by departmental personnel during the interview
    D. most closely resembles the atmosphere of the individual's personal life

6. Assume that you are interviewing a patient to determine whether he has any savings accounts.
   To obtain this information, the MOST effective way to phrase your question would be:
   A. "You don't have any savings, do you?"
   B. "At which bank do you have a savings account?"
   C. "Do you have a savings account?"
   D. "May I assume that you have a savings account?"

7. You are interviewing a patient who is not cooperating to the extent necessary to get all required information. Therefore, you decide to be more forceful in your approach.
   In this situation, such a course of action is
   A. *advisable*, because such a change in approach may help to increase the patient's participation
   B. *advisable*, because you will be using your authority more effectively
   C. *inadvisable*, because you will not be able to change this approach if it doesn't produce results
   D. *inadvisable*, because an aggressive approach generally reduces the validity of the interview

8. You have attempted to interview a patient on two separate occasions, and both attempts were unsuccessful. The patient has been totally uncooperative and you sense a personal hostility toward you.
   Of the following, the BEST way to handle this type of situation would be to
   A. speak to the patient in a courteous manner and ask him to explain exactly what he dislikes about you
   B. inform the patient that you will not allow personality conflicts to disrupt the interview
   C. make no further attempt to interview the patient and recommend that he be billed in full
   D. discuss the problem with your supervisor and suggest that another investigator be assigned to try to interview the patient

9. At the beginning of an interview, a patient with normal vision tells you that he is reluctant to discuss his finances. You realize that it will be necessary in this case to ask detailed questions about his net income.
   When you begin this line of questioning, of the following, the LEAST important aspect you should consider is your
   A. precise wording of the question   B. manner of questioning
   C. tone of voice   D. facial expressions

10. A caseworker under your supervision has been assigned the task of interviewing a man who is applying for foster home placement for his two children. The caseworker seeks your advice as to how to question this man, stating that she finds the applicant to be a timid and self-conscious person who seems torn between the necessity of having to answer the worker's questions truthfully and the effect he thinks his answers will have on his application.

Of the following, the BEST method for the caseworker to use in order to determine the essential facts in this case is to
- A. assure the applicant that he need not worry since the majority of applications for foster home placement are approved
- B. delay the applicant's narration of the facts important to the case until his embarrassment and fears have been overcome
- C. ignore the statements made by the applicant and obtain all the required information from his friends and relatives
- D. inform the applicant that all statements made by him will be verified and are subject to the law governing perjury

11. Assume that a worker is interviewing a boy in his assigned group in order to help him find a job.
    At the BEGINNING of the interview, the worker should
    - A. suggest a possible job for the youth
    - B. refer the youth to an employment agency
    - C. discuss the youth's work history and skills with him
    - D. refer the youth to the manpower and career development agency

12. As part of the investigation to locate an absent father, you make a field visit to interview one of the father's friends. Before beginning the interview, you identify yourself to the friend and show him your official identification.
    For you to do this is, generally,
    - A. *good practice*, because the friend will have proof that you are authorized to make such confidential investigations
    - B. *poor practice*, because the friend may not answer your questions when he knows why you are interviewing him
    - C. *good practice*, because your supervisor can confirm from the friend that you actually made the interview
    - D. *poor practice*, because the friend may warn the absent father that your agency is looking for him

13. You are interviewing a client in his home as part of your investigation of an anonymous complaint that he has been receiving Medicaid fraudulently.
    During the interview, the client frequently interrupts your questions to discuss the hardships of his life and the bitterness he feels about his medical condition.
    Of the following, the BEST way for you to deal with these discussions is to
    - A. cut them off abruptly, since the client is probably just trying to avoid answering your questions
    - B. listen patiently, since these discussions may be helpful to the client and may give you information for your investigation
    - C. remind the client that you are investigating a complaint against him and he must answer directly
    - D. seek to gain the client's confidence by discussing any personal or medical problems which you yourself may have

14. While interviewing an absent father to determine his ability to pay child support, you realize that his answers to some of your questions contradict his answers to other questions.
    Of the following, the BEST way for you to try to get accurate information from the father is to
    A. confront him with his contradictory answers and demand an explanation from him
    B. use your best judgment as to which of his answers are accurate and question him accordingly
    C. tell him that he has misunderstood your questions and that he must clarify his answers
    D. ask him the same questions in different words and follow up his answer with related questions

14.____

15. Assume that an applicant, obviously under a great deal of stress, talks continuously and rambles, making it difficult for you to determine the exact problem and her need.
    In order to make the interview more successful, it would be BEST for you to
    A. interrupt the applicant and ask her specific questions in order to get the information you need
    B. tell the applicant that her rambling may be a basic cause of her problem
    C. let the applicant continue talking as long as she wishes
    D. ask the applicant to get to the point because other people are waiting for you

15.____

16. A worker must be able to interview clients all day and still be able to listen and maintain interest.
    Of the following, it is MOST important for you to show interest in the client because, if you appear interested,
    A. the client is more likely to appreciate your professional status
    B. the client is more likely to disclose a greater amount of information
    C. the client is less likely to tell lie
    D. you are more likely to gain your supervisor's approval

16.____

17. When you are interviewing clients, it is important to notice and record how they say what they say—angrily, nervously, or with "body English"—because these signs may
    A. tell you that the client's words are the opposite of what the client feels and you may need to dig to find out what those feeling are
    B. be the prelude to violent behavior which no aide is prepared to handle
    C. show that the client does not really deserve serious consideration
    D. be important later should you be asked to defend what you did for the client

17.____

18. The patient you are interviewing is reticent and guarded in responding to your questions. He is not providing the information needed to complete his application for medical assistance.
    In this situation, the one of the following which is the MOST appropriate course of action for you to take FIRST is to

18.____

A. end the interview and ask him to contact you when he is ready to answer your questions
B. advise the patient that you cannot end the interview until he has provided all the information you need to complete the application
C. emphasize to the patient the importance of the questions and the need to answer them in order to complete the application
D. advise the patient that if he answers your questions the interview will be easier for both of you

19. At the end of an interview with a patient, he describes a problem he is having with his teenage son, who is often truant and may be using narcotics. The patient asks you for advice in handling his son.
Of the following, the MOST appropriate action for you to take is to
    A. make an appointment to see the patient and his son together
    B. give the patient a list of drug counseling programs to which he may refer his son
    C. suggest to the patient that his immediate concern should be his own hospitalization rather than his son's problem
    D. tell the patient that you are not qualified to assist him but will attempt to find out who can

20. A MOST appropriate condition in the use of direct questions to obtain personal data in an interview is that, whenever possible,
    A. the direct questions be used only as a means of encouraging the person interviewed to talk about himself
    B. provision be made for recording the information
    C. the direct questions be used only after all other methods have failed
    D. the person being interviewed understands the reason for requesting the information

KEY (CORRECT ANSWERS)

1.	D	11.	C
2.	A	12.	A
3.	A	13.	B
4.	D	14.	D
5.	A	15.	A
6.	B	16.	B
7.	A	17.	A
8.	D	18.	C
9.	A	19.	D
10.	B	20.	D

EXAMINATION SECTION
TEST 1

DIRECTIONS: Each question or incomplete statement is followed by several suggested answers or completions. Select the one that BEST answers the question or completes the statement. *PRINT THE LETTER OF THE CORRECT ANSWER IN THE SPACE AT THE RIGHT.*

Questions 1-4.

DIRECTIONS: Questions 1 through 4 are to be answered SOLELY on the basis of the following paragraph.

Although a few organizations have tended to thwart the inclination of their employees as human beings to develop and mature, to seek identity with their work and to seek higher ego satisfactions, there are ways to organize and direct endeavors so that these human inclinations are used to the advantage of both the worker and such organizations.

1. According to the paragraph, it is possible to arrange the activities of an organization so that employees can 1.____

    A. be paid according to their productivity
    B. become personally involved in their work
    C. have the same authority as management
    D. participate in group-think sessions

2. According to the paragraph, a few organizations, in dealing with employees, have been inclined to 2.____

    A. demand increased production
    B. frustrate human development
    C. organize for a maximum efficiency
    D. compel loyalty

3. According to the paragraph, positive human tendencies may successfully be employed to 3.____

    A. benefit both employees and employers
    B. develop new methods of training all workers
    C. overcome intergroup conflict
    D. promote cooperation between one organization and another

4. As used in the paragraph, the underlined word endeavors means MOST NEARLY 4.____

    A. efforts   B. personalities
    C. subordinates   D. talents

Questions 5-9.

DIRECTIONS: Questions 5 through 9 are to be answered SOLELY on the basis of the following paragraphs.

Known by many names, flexible working hours refers to a system whereby individual employees can come and go as they wish, within certain limits, so long as they work a prescribed number of hours each week. However, a problem which appears in the administration of the flexible working hour system is that of recording time.

One of the current developments in progressive management is the reduced use of the age-old time clock wherein employees are expected to punch in and out when they come to work and leave. Time clocks are seen as a symbol of control, of impersonality, of class distinction. To eliminate them would at least remove the symbol. By and large, it is believed that time clocks, although useful from an administrative point of view, are negative motivators.

5. According to the paragraph, an employee working a conventional work week of 37 1/2 hours would, if his employer adopted a system of flexible hours, MOST likely

   A. have a reduction in job duties
   B. come to work at an earlier hour
   C. work fewer total hours
   D. work 37 1/2 hours a week, as before

6. According to the paragraph, time clocks are

   A. a useful means of managerial control
   B. in favor among progressive organizations
   C. of little significance to employees
   D. the basic reason for flexible working hours

7. According to the paragraph, a problem exists in using time clocks in conjunction with a flexible working hours system CHIEFLY because

   A. employees may be unwilling to change their habits of working from 9 A.M. to 5 P.M.
   B. the increase in feelings of freedom would be adversely affected
   C. some managers feel that their authority is diminished
   D. the usual distinction between management and employees is blurred

8. According to the paragraph, under a system of flexible working hours, it might be DIFFICULT to

   A. obtain employee acceptance of a flexible time schedule
   B. reduce the authority of management
   C. record accurately employees' working time
   D. decrease administrative control over work

9. As used in the paragraph, the underlined word progressive means MOST NEARLY

   A. corporate   B. enlightened
   C. generous   D. technical

Questions 10-12.

DIRECTIONS: Questions 10 through 12 are to be answered SOLELY on the basis of the following paragraph.

There are two major and interrelated difficulties in evolving a pattern of federal-state-local relationships for dealing with drug abuse. First, the diversity among the states; second, the need for frequent innovation.

10. As used in the paragraph, the underlined word <u>evolving</u> means MOST NEARLY   10.____
    A. controlling   B. developing   C. measuring   D. predicting

11. As used in the paragraph, the underlined word <u>diversity</u> means MOST NEARLY   11.____
    A. problem   B. rights   C. structure   D. differences

12. As used in the paragraph, the underlined word <u>innovation</u> means MOST NEARLY   12.____
    A. change   B. evaluation   C. funding   D. planning

Questions 13-15.

DIRECTIONS: Questions 13 through 15 are to be answered SOLELY on the basis of the following paragraph.

One of the major problems facing the manager of the future is that of coping with increased sophistication in all aspects of managing. Of particular importance has been the introduction of newer techniques in the areas of management planning and control. These, based upon the systems approaches brought over from the physical sciences, include applications of such important techniques as operations research, network analysis, and the new information technologies. Likewise, there have been the many findings of the behavioral sciences which, if they can be intelligently applied to managing, can improve personal efficiency. Practice, however, has been slow to adopt many of these new techniques and findings. Most managers have not adopted them simply because they do not understand them. What individuals in a responsible position do not understand, they are not likely to trust or use. Much of this has arisen from the fact that experts in these fields seem to thrive on a kind of mysticism and jargon which protects their image as experts but which becomes unintelligible to most managers.

13. According to the paragraph, the new techniques of PARTICULAR importance to the manager of the future are derived from   13.____
    A. increased managerial sophistication
    B. systems approaches used in physical science
    C. intelligently applied managerial findings
    D. analysis of management problems by electrical engineers

14. According to the above paragraph, the manager who makes wise use of the findings of the behavioral sciences is MOST likely to   14.____
    A. make good use of the findings of the physical sciences
    B. influence his subordinates to be more careful employees
    C. increase his own effectiveness as a manager
    D. include technical specialists in operations analysis among his subordinates

15. According to the paragraph, many managers today do not quickly apply scientific innovations to managerial operations PRIMARILY because   15.____
    A. they are unaware of the need for innovation and improvement
    B. the benefits of change are delayed while the costs are immediate
    C. the innovations are too technical for most managers to grasp
    D. managerial jobs are often eliminated when scientific innovations are introduced

16. In order for employees to function effectively, they should have a feeling of being treated fairly by management. Which of the following general policies is MOST likely to give employees such a feeling?

    A. An employee publication should be mailed directly to the home of each employee.
    B. Employee attitude surveys should be conducted at regular intervals.
    C. Employees should be consulted and kept informed on all matters that affect them.
    D. Employees should be informed when the press publishes statements of policy.

17. In order to give employees in a human services organization greater job satisfaction, some management experts advocate a policy of job enrichment. The one of the following which would be the BEST example of job enrichment is to

    A. allow an aide to decide which portion of his normal duties and responsibilities he prefers
    B. increase the fringe benefits currently available to paraprofessional employees
    C. add variety to the duties of a specialist
    D. permit more flexible working schedules for professional employees

18. Management of large organizations has often emphasized high salaries and fringe benefits as the most important means of motivating employees. The one of the following which is NOT an argument used to support this approach is:

    A. Most people endure work mainly in order to collect the rewards and to have the opportunity to enjoy them
    B. Material incentives have proved to be the best means of stimulating creative capacity and the will to work
    C. The majority of employees place little emphasis on work-centered motivation to perform
    D. Numerous research studies have shown that pay ranks first on a scale of factors motivating employees in government and industry in the United States

19. Some organizations provide psychologists or other professionally trained persons with whom employees can consult on a confidential basis regarding personal problems. Of the following, which is MOST likely to be a benefit management can derive from such a practice?

    A. Increase in the authority of management
    B. Disclosure of the corrupt practices of those handling money
    C. Receipt of new ideas and approaches to organizational problems
    D. Obtaining tighter control on employees' private behavior

20. Authorities agree that it is generally most desirable for an employee experiencing mental health problems to seek competent professional help without being required or forced to do so by another person.
    They view self-referral as a most desirable action PRIMARILY because

    A. it shows that the employee probably is more aware of the problem and more highly motivated to solve his problems
    B. the employee's right to privacy in his personal affairs is maintained
    C. another person cannot be blamed in the event the outcome of the referral is not successful
    D. the employee knows best his problems and will do what is necessary to serve his own best interests

KEY (CORRECT ANSWERS)

1. B
2. B
3. A
4. A
5. D

6. A
7. B
8. C
9. B
10. B

11. D
12. A
13. B
14. C
15. C

16. C
17. C
18. D
19. C
20. A

TEST 2

DIRECTIONS: Each question or incomplete statement is followed by several suggested answers or completions. Select the one that BEST answers the question or completes the statement. *PRINT THE LETTER OF THE CORRECT ANSWER IN THE SPACE AT THE RIGHT.*

1. An inexperienced worker reports to his supervisor that he knows that a member of his assigned gang group is *packing,* but feels that it would be unethical to betray confidentiality by informing the police.
   The supervisor should

   A. tell the worker to take the weapon away from the youth and turn it over to the police
   B. call the youth into his office and order him to turn the weapon over to the police
   C. explain agency policy and the worker's responsibility to report information about illegal activity, and help the worker to overcome his concern about betraying the youth
   D. none of the above

2. While a supervisor is making a visit to the field, several members of a worker's assigned gang group tell him that the worker is never there and that they don't even know him. It is the worker's day off.
   The supervisor should first

   A. recommend that the worker be brought up on charges for being absent without permission
   B. realize that he should not believe what the group says, since they probably don't like the worker
   C. call the worker in for a conference and warn him that he will be disciplined for absence without permission
   D. make regular return visits to the field in order to investigate the situation

3. Of the following, the MOST important reason why a supervisor should devote a considerable part of his time to reading and reviewing workers' records of activities with their groups is in order to

   A. hold workers accountable for what they do with their groups
   B. use the records as tools to rate workers' performance
   C. obtain background information on the group members and their activities
   D. insure that the youths in the groups get proper and adequate service

4. Assume that a newly assigned worker reports to his supervisor that three of the members of his assigned group have asked him to buy a bottle of wine, and that he does not know what to do.
   The supervisor should

   A. consult with his unit supervisor before giving guidance to the worker on how to handle this situation
   B. tell the worker not to buy the wine, and clarify for the worker his role in setting appropriate standards of behavior
   C. tell the worker to decide how to handle this himself, because it is better for him to learn through experience
   D. visit the field with the worker in order to discuss the situation with the group of youths

5. Assume that a supervisor finds that one of his workers, who is three weeks behind in his recording, has a good relationship with his assigned group, seems to be helping then to become involved in constructive activities, but insists that he does not have time to keep up with his recording.
   The BEST method for the supervisor to use in order to get the worker to complete his recording on time is to

   A. send the worker a memorandum pointing out his responsibility for recording as a means of accountability
   B. take the worker to see the unit supervisor to discuss his problems about recording
   C. allow the worker to record at his own pace, since constructive contacts with youths are more important than records
   D. discuss importance of recording with the worker and help him make out a schedule in order to allow time for this part of his work

5.____

6. A supervisor receives a program request from a youth worker who wants to take his assigned group on a trip to Philadelphia, Pa., to see a non-violent anti-poverty demonstration at first hand.
   The supervisor should

   A. *disapprove* the trip, and advise the worker that it would be dangerous to take this group to such a demonstration, since they may provoke violence
   B. *approve* the trip, because it would be risky to take the group to such a demonstration if it took place in or near their own neighborhood
   C. *disapprove* the trip and advise the worker to try to reach the same goals and objectives by taking the group to a similar event which takes place in or near the city
   D. *approve* the trip, because the worker should be supported since he probably has already raised the expectations of the group

6.____

7. A supervisor has a new worker whose records indicate that he has potential for becoming an excellent staff member. However, when the supervisor observes the worker in the field, he notices that the worker frequently holds back and seems uncertain in handling his group. When the supervisor talks to the worker about this in private, the worker explains that he hesitates because he is *afraid of doing the wrong thing.*
   The BEST way for the supervisor to help this worker is to

   A. assign him to another group until he gets more experience
   B. suggest to him that he would feel better if he had professional training
   C. give him reassurance and as much guidance as he needs
   D. go into the field with him to work with his youths so he can learn directly from him

7.____

8. A youth worker informs his supervisor that he has to devote so much attention to one of his group members, who has a multitude of serious family and individual problems, that he cannot give enough time to the other members of the group.
   The supervisor should *advise* the worker to

   A. refer the youth to a casework agency for counseling and devote more of his time to the needs of the group as a whole
   B. work overtime, so that he can counsel the youth individually and also give proper attention to the group
   C. call a group meeting to elicit the help of the other gang members in helping this youth
   D. continue to give priority to counseling this youth, since his problems are so serious in nature and may otherwise come to a crisis

8.____

9. The supervisor is responsible for training and developing recently appointed youth workers who have been assigned to his unit.
   After orientation in the office, the MOST effective way for the supervisor to handle a worker's first field visit is for the supervisor to

   A. assign him to an experienced worker, who will introduce him to gang groups in the area
   B. send him out alone, so that he will develop confidence by making his own contacts
   C. accompany him, in order to introduce him to key people and explain his responsibilities while in the field
   D. send him out with letters of introduction to key staff members of youth-serving agencies and community leaders in his assigned area

10. In accepted practice, it is considered important for the supervisor to hold regular individual conferences with his youth workers.
    The MAJOR purpose of the *individual* supervisory conference is to

    A. make certain that the worker is properly indoctrinated in agency policies and procedures
    B. train the worker through discussion and analysis of his experience and problems with his assigned group
    C. gather data to use to properly evaluate the worker and protect the agency and the supervisor
    D. help the worker to analyze, clarify, and resolve his personal problems

11. Assume that an inexperienced worker phones his supervisor and informs him that his assigned group is about to *go down* on another group. This is the worker's first such experience.
    The supervisor's FIRST action should be to

    A. advise the worker not to alert the police but to keep him posted of further developments
    B. meet the worker in the field, and call the police himself if he finds that the worker has appraised the situation correctly
    C. advise the worker to *rap* with group members in an attempt to dissuade them from conflict, so that he will not have to call the police
    D. send an experienced worker to help the new worker handle the situation

12. An inexperienced youth worker informs his supervisor that members of his assigned group have threatened him with bodily harm, and that he is afraid to continue working with them.
    Which of the following actions should the supervisor take FIRST?

    A. Reassign the worker, since a supervisor should not unnecessarily risk a worker's life
    B. Immediately alert the police to the threats made to the youth worker by the gang members
    C. Visit the group and evaluate their feelings about the worker by means of a sensitivity session
    D. Discuss the situation further with the worker in an attempt to determine whether his fears are realistic

13. Of the following, the MOST important purpose of *regular* supervisory evaluations of workers' performance is to

    A. praise workers for superior performance
    B. help workers improve their performance by giving them an objective picture of their strengths and weaknesses
    C. give the supervisor an opportunity to discipline workers whose performance is poor
    D. provide a permanent record of workers' performance for reference in case of future inquiries

14. When the supervisor goes into the field to observe group activities, he should devote the MAJOR part of his time to

    A. checking on whether the worker is meeting regularly with his group
    B. looking for program clues in the group's behavior
    C. observing the worker's relationships with his group and its members
    D. finding out whether the worker is meeting group requests

15. *Tasting* is a method or technique that is often used by members of a gang group to

    A. challenge and examine the worker's authority and role
    B. identify with the worker
    C. demonstrate acceptance of the worker
    D. get the worker's help with problems at school

16. Assume that a supervisor has discovered that a worker brought marijuana into his group's clubhouse.
    The supervisor should FIRST

    A. report the situation to the local police precinct
    B. warn the worker that he will be discharged if he is found with drugs
    C. determine whether the worker has brough marijuana into the clubroom previously
    D. make a complete investigation and report his findings to the area director

17. A youth worker asks his supervisor for advice about how to handle a group member whom he suspects of having a switchblade knife in his possession.
    The *best* suggestion the supervisor can make is that the worker should FIRST

    A. watch the group member closely in order to determine whether he has a knife
    B. warn the members as a group that members carrying knives will be reported to the police
    C. try to discover what psychological meaning the knife has for the group member
    D. tell the group member firmly that carrying such a knife is illegal

18. During his initial contact with a gang group, the youth worker USUALLY finds that the group's attitude towards him is

    A. ambivalent   B. aggressively friendly
    C. hostile and rejecting   D. helpful

19. If an inexperienced youth worker seems to be particularly tense about going to the field because he senses impending trouble, it would be BEST for the supervisor to

   A. send a more experienced worker to the field with him to evaluate the situation
   B. give his assignment to a more experienced worker until the emergency situation subsides
   C. have the worker's assigned group meet him in the unit office
   D. notify the police of possible trouble in order to relieve the worker's anxiety

20. Whenever a supervisor tactfully suggests improvements in a youth worker's handling of group members, the worker reacts by becoming angry and, on occasion, has walked out of the office, slamming the door.
    The *best* of the following actions for the supervisor to take FIRST is to

   A. have a discussion with the worker about his difficulty in handling criticism
   B. have the worker transferred, after explaining the reasons
   C. warn the worker that he will be disciplined if he cannot control his temper
   D. send the worker written comments on his performance whenever possible

KEY (CORRECT ANSWERS)

1.	C	11.	B
2.	C	12.	D
3.	D	13.	B
4.	B	14.	C
5.	D	15.	A
6.	C	16.	D
7.	C	17.	A
8.	A	18.	C
9.	C	19.	A
10.	B	20.	A

EXAMINATION SECTION
TEST 1

DIRECTIONS: Each question or incomplete statement is followed by several suggested answers or completions. Select the one that BEST answers the question or completes the statement. *PRINT THE LETTER OF THE CORRECT ANSWER IN THE SPACE AT THE RIGHT.*

1. It is generally accepted that, of the following, the MOST important medium for developing integration and continuity in learning on the job is
   A. day-to-day experience on the job
   B. the supervisory conference
   C. the staff meeting
   D. the professional seminar

   1.____

2. Assume that you find that one of your workers is over-identifying with a particular client.
   Of the following, the MOST appropriate step for you to take FIRST in dealing with this situation is to
   A. transfer the cases to another worker
   B. inform the worker that he cannot give satisfactory service if he over-identifies with a client
   C. interview the client yourself to determine his feelings about his relationship with the worker
   D. arrange a conference with the worker to discuss the reasons for her over-identification with this client

   2.____

3. The one of the following which is the MOST likely reason why a newly-appointed supervisor would have a tendency to interfere actively in a relationship between one of his workers and a client is that the supervisor
   A. has unresolved feelings about relinquishing the role of worker, and has not yet accepted his role as supervisor
   B. must give direct assistance in the situation because the worker cannot handle it
   C. is attempting to share with his worker the knowledge and skill which he has developed in direct practice
   D. has not realized that immediate responsibility for work with clients has been delegated to others

   3.____

4. A worker who has a tendency to resist authority and supervision can be helped MOST effectively if, of the following, the supervisor
   A. behaves in a strict and impersonal manner so that the worker will accept his authority as a supervisor
   B. modifies the relationship so that he will be less authoritarian and threatening to the worker
   C. gives the worker a simple, matter-of-fact interpretation of the supervisory relationship and has an understanding acceptance of the worker's response
   D. temporarily establishes a peer relationship with the worker in order to overcome his resistance

   4.____

5. Before interviewing a newly-appointed worker for the first time, of the following, it is DESIRABLE for the supervisor to
   A. learn as much as he can about the worker's background and interests in order to eliminate the routine of asking questions and eliciting answers
   B. review the job information to be covered in order to make it easier to be impersonal and keep to the business at hand
   C. send the worker orientation material about the agency and the job and ask him to study it before the interview
   D. review available information about the worker in order to find an area of shared experience to serve as a *taking off* point for getting acquainted

6. In interviewing a new worker, of the following, it is IMPORTANT for the supervisor to
   A. give direction to the progress of the interview and maintain a leadership role throughout
   B. allow the worker to take the initiative in order to give him full scope for freedom of expression
   C. maintain a non-directional approach so that the worker will reveal his true attitudes and feelings
   D. avoid interrupting the worker, even though he seems to want to do all the talking

7. When a new worker, during his first few days, shows such symptoms of insecurity as *stage fright*, helpless immobility, or extreme talkativeness, of the following, it would be MOST helpful for the supervisor to
   A. start the worker out on some activity in which he is relatively secure
   B. ignore the symptoms and allow the worker to *sink or swim* on his own
   C. have a conference with the worker and interpret to him the reasons for his feelings of insecurity
   D. consider the probability that this worker may not be suited for a profession which requires skill in interpersonal relationships

8. Of the following, the MOST desirable method of minimizing workers' dependence on the supervisor and encouraging self-dependence is to
   A. hold group instead of individual supervisory conferences at regular intervals
   B. schedule individual supervisory conferences only in response to the workers' obvious need for guidance
   C. plan for progressive exposure to other opportunities for learning afforded by the agency and the community
   D. allow workers to learn by trial and error rather than by direct supervisory guidance

9. Of the following, it would NOT be appropriate for the supervisor to use early supervisory conferences with the new workers as a means of
   A. giving him direct practical help in order to get going on the job
   B. estimating the level of his native abilities, professional skills and experience
   C. getting clues as to his characteristic ways of learning in a new situation
   D. assessing his potential for future supervisory responsibility

10. Without careful planning by the supervisor for orientation of the new worker, an informal system of orientation by co-workers inevitably develops.
Such an informal system of orientation is USUALLY
    A. *beneficial*, because many new workers learn more readily when instructed by their peers
    B. *harmful*, because informal orientation by an undesignated co-worker can lead a new worker astray instead of helping him
    C. *beneficial*, because assumption by subordinates of responsibility for orientation will free the supervisor for other urgent work
    D. *harmful*, because such informal orientation by a co-worker will tend to destroy the authority of the supervisor

11. Of the following, the BEST way for a supervisor to assist a subordinate who has unusual work pressures is to
    A. relieve him of some of his cases until the pressures subside
    B. help him to decide which cases should be given the most attention during the period of pressure, and how to provide coverage for less urgent cases
    C. inform him that he must learn to tolerate and adjust to such pressures
    D. point out that he should learn to understand the causes of the pressures, which probably resulted from his own deficiencies

12. Many supervisors have a tendency to use case records mainly for the purpose of analysis of the workers' skill or evaluation of their performance.
Of the following, a PROBABLE result of this practice is that
    A. workers are likely to tie-in recording with supervisory evaluation of their work, without giving proper emphasis to their importance in improving service to clients
    B. the worker is likely to devote an inordinate amount of time to case records at the expense of his clients
    C. the records are likely to be too lengthy and detailed, limiting their value for other important purposes
    D. the records are likely to be of little value for administrative and research purposes

13. A common obstacle to adequate recording in a large social work agency is the fact that many workers consider recording to be a time-consuming chore. In order to obtain the cooperation of staff in keeping proper records, of the following, it is MOST important for an agency to provide
    A. indisputable evidence of the intelligent use of records as tools in formulating policy and improving service
    B. a system of checks and controls to assure that workers are preparing adequate and timely records
    C. adequate clerical services and mechanical equipment for recording
    D. sufficient time for recording in the organization of every job

14. The one of the following which is NOT a purpose of keeping case records in an agency is
    A. planning
    B. research
    C. training
    D. job classification

15. When a supervisor is reviewing the records of a worker, of the following, he should plan to read
    A. records of new cases only, following up each interview selectively
    B. the total caseload, in order to determine which aspects of the worker's performance should be examined
    C. those records which the worker has brought to the supervisor's attention because of the need for help
    D. a block of records selected according to the worker's need for help, and some records selected at random

16. The one of the following which is the PRIMARY purpose of the regular staff meeting in an agency is
    A. initiation of action in order to get the agency's work done
    B. staff training and development
    C. program and policy determination
    D. communication of new policies and procedures

17. Of the following, group supervision in an agency is intended as a means of
    A. strengthening the total supervisory process
    B. shifting the focus of supervision from the individual to the group
    C. saving costs in terms of time and manpower
    D. influencing policy through group interaction

18. The supervisor's job brings him closer to such limiting factors in the operation of an agency as faulty administrative structure, shortage of funds and lack of facilities, inadequacies in personnel practices, community pressures, and excessive workload.
    For the supervisor to make a practice of communicating to his subordinates his feelings of frustration about such limitations in the work setting would be
    A. *appropriate*, because the worker will be more understanding of the supervisor's burdens and frustrations
    B. *inappropriate*, because the climate created will block rather than further the purposes of supervision
    C. *appropriate*, because such communication will create a more democratic climate between the worker and the supervisor
    D. *inappropriate*, because the supervisor must support and condone agency policies and practices in the presence of subordinates

19. A suggestion has been made that the teaching and administrative functions of supervision should be separated, so that the supervisor responsible for teaching would not be responsible for evaluation of the same workers.
    The one of the following which is the MOST important reason for this point of view is that
    A. elements that confer on the supervisor a position of authority and power unduly threaten the learning situation
    B. teaching skill and administrative ability do not usually go together

C. a supervisor who has been responsible for training a worker is likely to be prejudiced in his favor
D. performance evaluation and total job accountability should be two separate functions

20. In reviewing a worker's cases in preparation for a periodic evaluation, you note that she has done a uniformly good job with certain types of cases and poor work with other types of cases.
Of the following, the BEST approach for you to take in this situation is to
    A. bring this to the worker's attention, find out why she favors certain types of clients, and discuss ways in which she can improve her service to all clients
    B. bring this to the worker's attention and suggest that she may need professional counseling, as she seems to be blocked in working with certain types of cases
    C. assign to her mainly those cases which she handles best and transfer the types of cases which she handles poorly to another worker
    D. accept the fact that a worker cannot be expected to give uniformly good service to all clients, and take no further action

20.____

KEY (CORRECT ANSWERS)

1.	B	11.	B
2.	D	12.	A
3.	A	13.	A
4.	C	14	D
5.	D	15.	D
6.	A	16.	A
7.	A	17.	A
8.	C	18.	B
9.	D	19.	A
10.	B	20.	A

TEST 2

DIRECTIONS: Each question or incomplete statement is followed by several suggested answers or completions. Select the one that BEST answers the question or completes the statement. *PRINT THE LETTER OF THE CORRECT ANSWER IN THE SPACE AT THE RIGHT.*

1. Of the following, the choice of method to be used in the supervisory process should be influenced MOST by the
   A. number and type of cases carried by each worker
   B. emotional maturity of the worker
   C. number of workers supervised and their past experience
   D. subject matter to be learned and the long-range goals of supervision

   1.____

2. In an evaluation conference with a worker, the BEST approach for the supervisor to take is to
   A. help the worker to identify his strengths as a basis for working on his weaknesses
   B. identify the worker's weaknesses and help him overcome them
   C. allow the worker to identify his weaknesses first and then suggest ways of overcoming them
   D. discuss the worker's weaknesses but emphasize his strengths

   2.____

3. Assume that a worker is discouraged about the progress of his work and feels that it is futile to attempt to cope with many of his cases.
   Of the following, it would be BEST for the supervisor to
   A. suggest to the worker that such feelings are inappropriate for a professional worker
   B. tell the worker that he must seek professional help in order to overcome these feelings
   C. reduce the worker's caseload and give him cases that are less complex
   D. review with the worker several of his cases in which there were obvious accomplishments

   3.____

4. The supervisor is responsible for providing the worker with the following means of support, with the EXCEPTION of
   A. interest and advice on his personal problems
   B. instruction on community resources
   C. inspiration for carrying out the work of the agency
   D. understanding his strengths and limitations

   4.____

5. When a worker frequently takes the initiative in asking questions and discussing problems during a supervisory conference, this is PROBABLY an indication that the
   A. supervisor is not sufficiently interested in the work
   B. conference is a positive learning experience for the worker
   C. worker is hostile and resists supervision
   D. supervisor's position of authority is in question

   5.____

6. When a supervisor finds that one of his workers cannot accept criticism, of the following, it would be BEST for the supervisor to
   A. have the worker transferred to another supervisor
   B. warn the worker of disciplinary proceedings unless his attitude changes
   C. have the worker suspended after explaining the reason
   D. explore with the worker his attitude toward authority

7. Of the following, the condition which the inexperienced worker is LEAST likely to be aware of, without the guidance of the supervisor, is
   A. when he is successful in helping a client
   B. when he is not making progress in helping a client
   C. that he has a personal bias toward certain clients
   D. that he feels insecure because of lack of experience

8. The supervisor should provide an inexperienced worker with controls as well as freedom MAINLY because controls will
   A. enable him to set up his own controls sooner
   B. put him in a situation which is closer to the realities of life
   C. help him to use authority in handling a casework problem
   D. give him a feeling of security and lay the foundation for future self-direction

9. A result of the use of summarized case recording by the worker is that it
   A. gives the supervisor more responsibility for selecting cases to discuss in conference
   B. makes more time available for other activities
   C. lowers the morale of many workers
   D. decreases discussion of cases by the worker and the supervisor

10. The distinction between the role of professional workers and the role of auxiliary or sub-professional workers in an agency is based upon the
    A. position within the agency hierarchy
    B. amount of close supervision given
    C. emergent nature of tasks assigned
    D. functions performed

11. Of the following, the MOST important source of learning for the worker should be
    A. departmental directives and professional literature
    B. his co-workers in the agency
    C. the content of in-service training courses
    D. the clients in his caseload

12. A client is MOST likely to feel that he is receiving acceptance and understanding if the social worker
    A. gets detailed information about the client's problem
    B. demonstrates that he realistically understands the client's problem
    C. has an intellectual understanding of the client's problem
    D. offers the client assurance of assistance

13. A client will be MORE encouraged to speak freely about his problems if the worker
    A. avoids asking too many questions
    B. asks leading rather than pointed questions
    C. suggests possible answers
    D. identifies with the client

14. A client would be MOST likely to be able to accept help in a time of crisis and need if the worker
    A. explains agency policy to him
    B. responds immediately to the client's need
    C. explains why help cannot be given immediately
    D. reaches out to help the client establish his rightful claim for assistance

15. It is a generally accepted principle that the worker should interpret for himself what the client is saying, but usually should not pass his interpretation on to the client because the client
    A. will become hostile to the worker
    B. should arrive at his own conclusions at his own pace
    C. must request the interpretation first
    D. usually wants facts, rather than the worker's interpretation

16. In evaluating the client's capacity to cope with his problems, it is MOST important for the worker to assess his ability to
    A. form close relationships
    B. ask for help
    C. express his hostility
    D. verbalize his difficulties

17. When a worker finds that he disagrees strongly with an agency policy, it is DESIRABLE for him to
    A. share his feelings about the policy with his client
    B. understand fully why he has such strong feelings about the policy
    C. refer cases involving the policy to his supervisor
    D. refuse to give help in cases involving the policy

18. Which of the following practices is BEST for a supervisor to use when assigning work to his staff?
    A. Give workers with seniority the most difficult jobs
    B. Assign all unimportant work to the slower workers
    C. Permit each employee to pick the job he prefers
    D. Make assignments based on the workers' abilities

19. In which of the following instances is a supervisor MOST justified in giving commands to people under his supervision?
    When
    A. they delay in following instructions which have been given to them clearly
    B. they become relaxed and slow about work, and he wants to speed up their production
    C. he must direct them in an emergency situation
    D. he is instructing them on jobs that are unfamiliar to them

20. Which of the following supervisory actions or attitudes is MOST likely to result in getting subordinates to try to do as much work as possible for a supervisor?
    He
    A. shows that his most important interest is in schedules and production goals
    B. consistently pressures his staff to get the work out
    C. never fails to let them know he is in charge
    D. considers their abilities and needs while requiring that production goals be met

20.____

KEY (CORRECT ANSWERS)

1.	D	11.	D
2.	A	12.	B
3.	D	13.	D
4.	A	14	D
5.	B	15.	B
6.	D	16.	A
7.	C	17.	B
8.	D	18.	D
9.	B	19.	C
10.	D	20.	D

TEST 3

DIRECTIONS: Each question or incomplete statement is followed by several suggested answers or completions. Select the one that BEST answers the question or completes the statement. *PRINT THE LETTER OF THE CORRECT ANSWER IN THE SPACE AT THE RIGHT.*

1. One of your workers comes to you and complains in an angry manner about your having chosen him for some particular assignment. In your opinion, the subject of the complaint is trivial land unimportant, but it seems to be quite important to your worker.
   The BEST of the following actions for you to take in this situation is to
   A. allow the worker to continue talking until he has calmed down and then explain the reasons for your having chosen him for that particular assignment
   B. warn the worker to moderate his tone of voice at once because he is bordering on insubordination
   C. tell the worker in a friendly tone that he is making a tremendous fuss over an extremely minor matter
   D. point out to the worker that you are his immediate supervisor and that you are running the unit in accordance with official policy

   1.____

2. The one of the following which is the LEAST desirable action for an assistant supervisor to take in disciplining a subordinate for an infraction of the rules is to
   A. caution him against repetition of the infraction, even if it is minor
   B. point out his progress in applying the rules at the same time that you reprimand him
   C. be as specific as possible in reprimanding him for rule infractions
   D. allow a cooling-off period to elapse before reprimanding him

   2.____

3. A training program for workers assigned to the intake section should include actual practice in simulated interviews under simulated conditions.
   The one of the following educational principles which is the CHIEF justification for this statement is that
   A. the workers will remember what they see better and longer than what they read or hear
   B. the workers will learn more effectively by actually doing the act themselves than they would learn from watching others do it
   C. the conduct of simulated interviews once or twice will enable them to cope with the real situation with little difficulty
   D. a training program must employ methods of a practical nature if the workers are to find anything of lasting value in it

   3.____

4. In order for a supervisor to employ the system of democratic leadership in his supervision, it would generally be BEST for him to
   A. allow his subordinates to assist in deciding on methods of work performance and job assignments but only in those areas where decisions have not been made on higher administrative levels

   4.____

B. allow his subordinates to decide how to do the required work, interposing his authority when work is not completed on schedule or is improperly completed
C. attempt to make assignments of work to individuals only of the type which they enjoy doing
D. maintain control over job assignment and work production, but allow the subordinates to select methods of work and internal conditions of work at democratically conducted staff conferences

5. In a unit in which supervision has been considered quite effective, it has become necessary to press for above-normal production for a limited period to achieve a required goal.
The one of the following which is a LEAST likely result of this pressure is that
    A. there will be more *griping* by employees
    B. some workers will do both more and better work than has been normal for them
    C. there will be an enhanced feeling of group unity
    D. there will be increased absenteeism

6. For a supervisor to encourage competitive feelings among his staff is
    A. *advisable*, chiefly because the workers will perform more efficiently when they have proper motivation
    B. *inadvisable*, chiefly because the workers will not perform well under the pressure of competition
    C. *advisable*, chiefly because the workers will have a greater incentive to perform their job properly
    D. *inadvisable*, chiefly because the workers may focus their attention on areas where they excel and neglect other essential aspects of the job

7. In selecting jobs to be assigned to a new worker, the supervisor should assign those jobs which
    A. give the worker the greatest variety of experience
    B. offer the worker the greatest opportunity to achieve concrete results
    C. present the worker with the greatest stimulation because of their interesting nature
    D. require the least amount of contact with outside agencies

8. A supervisor should avoid a detailed discussion of a worker-client interview with a new worker before the worker has fully recorded the interview CHIEFLY because such a discussion might
    A. cover matters which are already fully covered and explained in the written record
    B. make the worker forget some important deal learned during the interview
    C. color the recording according to the worker's reaction to his supervisor's opinions
    D. minimize the worker's feeling of having reached a decision independently

9. Some supervisors encourage their worker to submit a list of their questions about specific jobs or their comments about problems they wish to discuss in advance of the worker-supervisor conference.
This practice is
    A. *desirable*, chiefly because it helps to stimulate and focus the worker's thinking about his caseload
    B. *undesirable*, chiefly because it will stifle the worker's free expression of his problems and attitudes
    C. *desirable,* chiefly because it will allow the conference to move along more smoothly and quickly
    D. *undesirable*, chiefly because it will restrict the scope of the conference and the variety of jobs discussed

10. An alert supervisor hears a worker apparently giving the wrong information to a client and immediately reprimands him severely.
For the supervisor to reprimand the worker at his point is poor CHIEFLY because
    A. instruction must precede correct performance
    B. oral reprimands are less effective than written reprimands
    C. the worker was given no opportunity to explain his reasons for what he did
    D. more effective training can be obtained by discussing the errors with a group of workers

11. The one of the following circumstances when it would generally be MOST proper for a supervisor to do a job himself rather than to train a subordinate to do the job is when it is
    A. a job which the supervisor enjoys doing and does well
    B. not a very time-consuming job but an important one
    C. difficult to train another to do the job, yet is not difficult for the supervisor to do
    D. unlikely that this or any similar job will have to be done again at any future time

12. Effective training of subordinates requires that the supervisor understand certain facts about learning and forgetting processes.
Among these is the fact that people GENERALLY
    A. forget what they learned at a much greater rate during the first day than during subsequent periods
    B. both learn and forget at a relatively constant rate and this rate is dependent upon their general intellectual capacity
    C. learn at a relatively constant rate except for periods of assimilation when the quantity of retained learning decreases while information is becoming firmly fixed in the mind
    D. learn very slowly at first when introduced to a new topic, after which there is a great increase in the rate of learning

13. It has been suggested that a subordinate who likes his superior will tend to do better work than one who does not.
    According to the MOST widely held current theories of supervision, this suggestion is a
    A. *bad* one, since personal relationships tend to interfere with proper professional relationships
    B. *bad* one, since the strongest motivating factors are fear and uncertainty
    C. *good* one, since liking one's superior is a motivating factor for good work performance
    D. *good* one, since liking one's supervisor is the most important factor in employee performance

14. One factor which might be given consideration in deciding upon the optimum span of control of a supervisor over his immediate subordinates is the position of the supervisor in the hierarchy of the organization.
    It is generally considered proper that the number of subordinates immediately supervised by a higher, upper echelon supervisor _____ the number supervised by lower level supervisors.
    A. is unrelated to and tends to form no pattern with
    B. should be about the same as
    C. should be larger than
    D. should be smaller than

15. The one of the following instances when it is MOST important for an upper level supervisor to follow the chain of command is when he is
    A. communicating decisions
    B. communicating information
    C. receiving suggestions
    D. seeking information

16. At the end of his probationary period, a supervisor should be considered potentially valuable in his position if he shows
    A. awareness of his areas of strength and weakness, identification with the administration of the department, and ability to learn under supervision
    B. skill in work, supervision, and administration, and a friendly democratic approach to the staff
    C. knowledge of departmental policies and procedures and ability to carry them out, ability to use authority, and ability to direct the work of the staff
    D. an identification with the department, acceptance of responsibility, and ability to give help to the individuals who are to be supervised

17. Good supervision is selective because
    A. it is not necessary to direct all the activities of the person
    B. a supervisor would never have time to know the whole caseload of a worker
    C. workers resent too much help from a supervisor
    D. too much reading is a waste of valuable time

18. An important administrative problem is how precisely to define the limits of authority that is delegated to subordinate supervisors.
Such definition of limits of authority should be
   A. as precise as possible and practicable in all areas
   B. as precise as possible and practicable in areas of function, but should allow considerable flexibility in the area of personnel management
   C. as precise as possible and practicable in the area
   D. of personnel management, but should allow considerable flexibility in the areas of function
   E. in general terms so as to allow considerable flexibility both in the areas of function and in the areas of personnel management

18.____

19. Experts in the field of personnel relations feel that it is generally a bad practice for subordinate employees to become aware of pending or contemplated changes in policy or organizational set-up via the *grapevine* CHIEFLY because
   A. evidence that one or more responsible officials have proved untrustworthy will undermine confidence in the agency
   B. the information disseminated by this method is seldom entirely accurate and generally spreads needless unrest among the subordinate staff
   C. the subordinate staff may conclude that the administration feels the staff cannot be trusted with the true information
   D. the subordinate staff may conclude that the administration lacks the courage to make an unpopular announcement through official channels

19.____

20. Supervision is subject to many interpretations, depending on the area in which it functions.
Of the following, the statement which represents the MOST appropriate meaning of supervision as it is known in social work practice is that it
   A. is a leadership process for the development of new leaders
   B. is an educational and administrative process aimed at teaching personnel the goal of improved service to the client
   C. is an activity aimed chiefly at insuring that workers will adhere to all agency directives
   D. provides the opportunity for administration to secure staff reaction to agency policies

20.____

21. A supervisor may utilize various methods in the supervisory process.
The one of the following upon which sound supervisory practice rests in the selection of supervisory techniques is
   A. an estimate of the worker arrived at through current and past evaluation of performance as well as through worker's participation
   B. the previous supervisor's evaluation and recommendation
   C. the worker's expression of his personal preference for certain types of experience
   D. the amount of time available to supervisor and supervisee

21.____

22. It is the practice of some supervisors, when they believe that it would be desirable for a subordinate to take a particular action in a case, to inform the subordinate of this in the form of a suggestion rather than in the form of a direct order.
In general, this method of getting a subordinate to take the desired action is
    A. *inadvisable*; it may create in the mind of the subordinate the impression that the supervisor is uncertain about the efficacy of her plan and is trying to avoid whatever responsibility she may have in resolving the case
    B. *advisable*; it provides the subordinate with the maximum opportunity to use her own judgment in handling the case
    C. *inadvisable*; it provides the subordinate with no clear-cut direction and, therefore, is likely to leave her with a feeling of uncertainty and frustration
    D. *advisable*; it presents the supervisor's view in a manner which will be most likely to evoke the subordinate's cooperation

22.____

23. A veteran supervisor noticed that one of her workers of average ability had begun developing some bad work habits, becoming especially careless in her recordkeeping. After reprimand from the supervisor, the investigator corrected her errors and has been doing satisfactory work since then.
For the supervisor to keep referring to this period of poor work during her weekly conferences with this employee would generally be considered poor personnel practice CHIEFLY because
    A. praise rather than criticism is generally the best method to use in improving the work of an unsatisfactory worker
    B. the supervisor cannot know whether the employee's errors will follow an established pattern
    C. the fault which evoked the original negative criticism no longer exists
    D. this would tend to frustrate the worker by making her strive overly hard to reach a level of productivity which is beyond her ability to achieve

23.____

24. Assume that you are now a supervisor in a specific unit. Two experienced investigators in your unit, both of whom do above average work, have for some time not gotten along with each other for personal reasons Their attitude toward one another has suddenly become hostile and noisy disagreement has taken place in the office.
The BEST action for you to take FIRST in this situation is to
    A. transfer one of the two investigators to another unit where contact with the other investigator will be unnecessary
    B. discuss the problem with the two investigators together, insisting that they confide in you and tell you the cause of their mutual antagonism
    C. confer with the two investigators separately, pointing out to each the need to adopt an adult professional attitude with respect to their on-the-job relations
    D. advise the two investigators that should the situation grow worse, disciplinary action will be considered

24.____

25. It has long been recognized that relationships exist between worker morale and working conditions.
 The one of the following which BEST clarifies these existing relationships is that morale is
 A. affected for better or worse in direct relationship to the magnitude of the changes in working conditions for better or worse
 B. better when working conditions are better
 C. little affected by working conditions so long as the working conditions do not approach the intolerable
 D. more affected by the degree of interest shown in providing good working conditions than by the actual conditions and may, perversely, be highest when working conditions are worst

25._____

KEY (CORRECT ANSWERS)

1.	A	11.	D
2.	D	12.	A
3.	B	13.	C
4.	A	14.	D
5.	D	15.	A
6.	D	16.	D
7.	B	17.	A
8.	C	18.	A
9.	A	19.	B
10.	C	20.	B

21. A
22. D
23. C
24. C
25. D

PHILOSOPHY, PRINCIPLES, PRACTICES, AND TECHNICS
OF
SUPERVISION, ADMINISTRATION, MANAGEMENT, AND ORGANIZATION

TABLE OF CONTENTS

	Page
MEANING OF SUPERVISION	1
THE OLD AND THE NEW SUPERVISION	1
THE EIGHT (8) BASIC PRINCIPLES OF THE NEW SUPERVISION	1
I. Principle of Responsibility	1
II. Principle of Authority	2
III. Principle of Self-Growth	2
IV. Principle of Individual Worth	2
V. Principle of Creative Leadership	2
VI. Principle of Success and Failure	2
VII. Principle of Science	3
VIII. Principle of Cooperation	3
WHAT IS ADMINISTRATION?	3
I. Practices Commonly Classed as "Supervisory"	3
II. Practices Commonly Classed as "Administrative"	3
III. Practices Commonly Classed as Both "Supervisory" and "Administrative"	4
RESPONSIBILITIES OF THE SUPERVISOR	4
COMPETENCIES OF THE SUPERVISOR	4
THE PROFESSIONAL SUPERVISOR-EMPLOYEE RELATIONSHIP	4
MINI-TEXT IN SUPERVISION, ADMINISTRATION, MANAGEMENT, AND ORGANIZATION	5
I. Brief Highlights	5
A. Levels of Management	6
B. What the Supervisor Must Learn	6
C. A Definition of Supervision	6
D. Elements of the Team Concept	6
E. Principles of Organization	6
F. The Four Important Parts of Every Job	7
G. Principles of Delegation	7
H. Principles of Effective Communications	7
I. Principles of Work Improvement	7
J. Areas of Job Improvement	7
K. Seven Key Points in Making Improvements	8

L.	Corrective Techniques for Job Improvement	8
M.	A Planning Checklist	8
N.	Five Characteristics of Good Directions	9
O.	Types of Directions	9
P.	Controls	9
Q.	Orienting the New Employee	9
R.	Checklist for Orienting New Employees	9
S.	Principles of Learning	10
T.	Causes of Poor Performance	10
U.	Four Major Steps in On-the-Job Instructions	10
V.	Employees Want Five Things	10
W.	Some Don'ts in Regard to Praise	11
X.	How to Gain Your Workers' Confidence	11
Y.	Sources of Employee Problems	11
Z.	The Supervisor's Key to Discipline	11
AA.	Five Important Processes of Management	12
BB.	When the Supervisor Fails to Plan	12
CC.	Fourteen General Principles of Management	12
DD.	Change	12

II. Brief Topical Summaries — 13
   A. Who/What is the Supervisor? — 13
   B. The Sociology of Work — 13
   C. Principles and Practices of Supervision — 14
   D. Dynamic Leadership — 14
   E. Processes for Solving Problems — 15
   F. Training for Results — 15
   G. Health, Safety, and Accident Prevention — 16
   H. Equal Employment Opportunity — 16
   I. Improving Communications — 16
   J. Self-Development — 17
   K. Teaching and Training — 17
      1. The Teaching Process — 17
         a. Preparation — 17
         b. Presentation — 18
         c. Summary — 18
         d. Application — 18
         e. Evaluation — 18
      2. Teaching Methods — 18
         a. Lecture — 18
         b. Discussion — 18
         c. Demonstration — 19
         d. Performance — 19
         e. Which Method to Use — 19

PHILOSOPHY, PRINCIPLES, PRACTICES, AND TECHNICS OF SUPERVISION, ADMINISTRATION, MANAGEMENT, AND ORGANIZATION

MEANING OF SUPERVISION

The extension of the democratic philosophy has been accompanied by an extension in the scope of supervision. Modern leaders and supervisors no longer think of supervision in the narrow sense of being confined chiefly to visiting employees, supplying materials, or rating the staff. They regard supervision as being intimately related to all the concerned agencies of society, they speak of the supervisor's function in terms of "growth," rather than the "improvement" of employees.

This modern concept of supervision may be defined as follows: Supervision is leadership and the development of leadership within groups which are cooperatively engaged in inspection, research, training, guidance, and evaluation.

THE OLD AND THE NEW SUPERVISION

TRADITIONAL
1. Inspection
2. Focused on the employee
3. Visitation
4. Random and haphazard
5. Imposed and authoritarian
6. One person usually

MODERN
1. Study and analysis
2. Focused on aims, materials, methods, supervisors, employees, environment
3. Demonstrations, intervisitation, workshops, directed reading, bulletins, etc.
4. Definitely organized and planned (scientific)
5. Cooperative and democratic
6. Many persons involved (creative)

THE EIGHT (8) BASIC PRINCIPLES OF THE NEW SUPERVISION

I. Principle of Responsibility
   Authority to act and responsibility for acting must be joined.
   A. If you give responsibility, give authority.
   B. Define employee duties clearly.
   C. Protect employees from criticism by others.
   D. Recognize the rights as well as obligations of employees.
   E. Achieve the aims of a democratic society insofar as it is possible within the area of your work.
   F. Establish a situation favorable to training and learning.
   G. Accept ultimate responsibility for everything done in your section, unit, office, division, department.
   H. Good administration and good supervision are inseparable.

II. Principle of Authority
The success of the supervisor is measured by the extent to which the power of authority is not used.
   A. Exercise simplicity and informality in supervision
   B. Use the simplest machinery of supervision
   C. If it is good for the organization as a whole, it is probably justified.
   D. Seldom be arbitrary or authoritative.
   E. Do not base your work on the power of position or of personality.
   F. Permit and encourage the free expression of opinions.

III. Principle of Self-Growth
The success of the supervisor is measured by the extent to which, and the speed with which, he is no longer needed.
   A. Base criticism on principles, not on specifics.
   B. Point out higher activities to employees.
   C. Train for self-thinking by employees to meet new situations.
   D. Stimulate initiative, self-reliance, and individual responsibility
   E. Concentrate on stimulating the growth of employees rather than on removing defects.

IV. Principle of Individual Worth
Respect for the individual is a paramount consideration in supervision.
   A. Be human and sympathetic in dealing with employees.
   B. Don't nag about things to be done.
   C. Recognize the individual differences among employees and seek opportunities to permit best expression of each personality.

V. Principle of Creative Leadership
The best supervision is that which is not apparent to the employee.
   A. Stimulate, don't drive employees to creative action.
   B. Emphasize doing good things.
   C. Encourage employees to do what they do best.
   D. Do not be too greatly concerned with details of subject or method.
   E. Do not be concerned exclusively with immediate problems and activities.
   F. Reveal higher activities and make them both desired and maximally possible.
   G. Determine procedures in the light of each situation but see that these are derived from a sound basic philosophy.
   H. Aid, inspire, and lead so as to liberate the creative spirit latent in all good employees.

VI. Principle of Success and Failure
There are no unsuccessful employees, only unsuccessful supervisors who have failed to give proper leadership.
   A. Adapt suggestions to the capacities, attitudes, and prejudices of employees.
   B. Be gradual, be progressive, be persistent.
   C. Help the employee find the general principle; have the employee apply his own problem to the general principle.
   D. Give adequate appreciation for good work and honest effort.
   E. Anticipate employee difficulties and help to prevent them.
   F. Encourage employees to do the desirable things they will do anyway.
   G. Judge your supervision by the results it secures.

VII. Principle of Science
Successful supervision is scientific, objective, and experimental. It is based on facts, not on prejudices.
   A. Be cumulative in results.
   B. Never divorce your suggestions from the goals of training.
   C. Don't be impatient of results.
   D. Keep all matters on a professional, not a personal, level.
   E. Do not be concerned exclusively with immediate problems and activities.
   F. Use objective means of determining achievement and rating where possible.

VIII. Principle of Cooperation
Supervision is a cooperative enterprise between supervisor and employee.
   A. Begin with conditions as they are.
   B. Ask opinions of all involved when formulating policies.
   C. Organization is as good as its weakest link.
   D. Let employees help to determine policies and department programs.
   E. Be approachable and accessible—physically and mentally.
   F. Develop pleasant social relationships.

WHAT IS ADMINISTRATION

Administration is concerned with providing the environment, the material facilities, and the operational procedures that will promote the maximum growth and development of supervisors and employees. (Organization is an aspect and a concomitant of administration.)

There is no sharp line of demarcation between supervision and administration; these functions are intimately interrelated and, often, overlapping. They are complementary activities.

I. Practices Commonly Classed as "Supervisory"
   A. Conducting employees' conferences
   B. Visiting sections, units, offices, divisions, departments
   C. Arranging for demonstrations
   D. Examining plans
   E. Suggesting professional reading
   F. Interpreting bulletins
   G. Recommending in-service training courses
   H. Encouraging experimentation
   I. Appraising employee morale
   J. Providing for intervisitation

II. Practices Commonly Classified as "Administrative"
   A. Management of the office
   B. Arrangement of schedules for extra duties
   C. Assignment of rooms or areas
   D. Distribution of supplies
   E. Keeping records and reports
   F. Care of audio-visual materials
   G. Keeping inventory records
   H. Checking record cards and books

I. Programming special activities
   J. Checking on the attendance and punctuality of employees

III. Practices Commonly Classified as Both "Supervisory" and "Administrative"
   A. Program construction
   B. Testing or evaluating outcomes
   C. Personnel accounting
   D. Ordering instructional materials

RESPONSIBILITIES OF THE SUPERVISOR

A person employed in a supervisory capacity must constantly be able to improve his own efficiency and ability. He represent the employer to the employees and only continuous self-examination can make him a capable supervisor.

Leadership and training are the supervisor's responsibility. An efficient working unit is one in which the employees work with the supervisor. It is his job to bring out the best in his employees. He must always be relaxed, courteous, and calm in his association with his employees. Their feelings are important, and a harsh attitude does not develop the most efficient employees.

COMPETENCES OF THE SUPERVISOR

   I. Complete knowledge of the duties and responsibilities of his position.
   II. To be able to organize a job, plan ahead, and carry through.
   III. To have self-confidence and initiative.
   IV. To be able to handle the unexpected situation and make quick decisions.
   V. To be able to properly train subordinates in the positions they are best suited for.
   VI. To be able to keep good human relations among his subordinates.
   VII. To be able to keep good human relations between his subordinates and himself and to earn their respect and trust.

THE PROFESSIONAL SUPERVISOR-EMPLOYEE RELATIONSHIP

There are two kinds of efficiency: one kind is only apparent and is produced in organizations through the exercise of mere discipline; this is but a simulation of the second, or true, efficiency which springs from spontaneous cooperation. If you are a manager, no matter how great or small your responsibility, it is your job, in the final analysis, to create and develop this involuntary cooperation among the people whom you supervise. For, no matter how powerful a combination of money, machines, and materials a company may have, this is a dead and sterile thing without a team of willing, thinking, and articulate people to guide it.

The following 21 points are presented as indicative of the exemplary basic relationship that should exist between supervisor and employee:

1. Each person wants to be liked and respected by his fellow employee and wants to be treated with consideration and respect by his superior.
2. The most competent employee will make an error. However, in a unit where good relations exist between the supervisor and his employees, tenseness and fear do not exist. Thus, errors are not hidden or covered up, and the efficiency of a unit is not impaired.

3. Subordinates resent rules, regulations, or orders that are unreasonable or unexplained.
4. Subordinates are quick to resent unfairness, harshness, injustices, and favoritism.
5. An employee will accept responsibility if he knows that he will be complimented for a job well done, and not too harshly chastised for failure; that his supervisor will check the cause of the failure, and, if it was the supervisor's fault, he will assume the blame therefore. If it was the employee's fault, his supervisor will explain the correct method or means of handling the responsibility.
6. An employee wants to receive credit for a suggestion he has made, that is used. If a suggestion cannot be used, the employee is entitled to an explanation. The supervisor should not say "no" and close the subject.
7. Fear and worry slow up a worker's ability. Poor working environment can impair his physical and mental health. A good supervisor avoids forceful methods, threats, and arguments to get a job done.
8. A forceful supervisor is able to train his employees individually and as a team, and is able to motivate them in the proper channels.
9. A mature supervisor is able to properly evaluate his subordinates and to keep them happy and satisfied.
10. A sensitive supervisor will never patronize his subordinates.
11. A worthy supervisor will respect his employees' confidences.
12. Definite and clear-cut responsibilities should be assigned to each executive.
13. Responsibility should always be coupled with corresponding authority.
14. No change should be made in the scope or responsibilities of a position without a definite understanding to that effect on the part of all persons concerned.
15. No executive or employee, occupying a single position in the organization, should be subject to definite orders from more than one source.
16. Orders should never be given to subordinates over the head of a responsible executive. Rather than do this, the officer in question should be supplanted.
17. Criticisms of subordinates should, whoever possible, be made privately, and in no case should a subordinate be criticized in the presence of executives or employees of equal or lower rank.
18. No dispute or difference between executives or employees as to authority or responsibilities should be considered too trivial for prompt and careful adjudication.
19. Promotions, wage changes, and disciplinary action should always be approved by the executive immediately superior to the one directly responsible.
20. No executive or employee should ever be required, or expected, to be at the same time an assistant to, and critic of, another.
21. Any executive whose work is subject to regular inspection should, wherever practicable, be given the assistance and facilities necessary to enable him to maintain an independent check of the quality of his work.

MINI-TEXT IN SUPERVISION, ADMINISTRATION, MANAGEMENT, AND ORGANIZATION

I. Brief Highlights

Listed concisely and sequentially are major headings and important data in the field for quick recall and review.

A. Levels of Management
Any organization of some size has several levels of management. In terms of a ladder, the levels are:

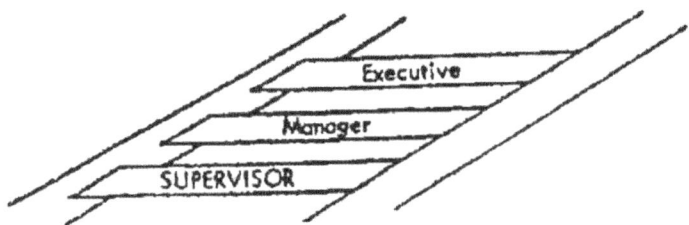

The first level is very important because it is the beginning point of management leadership.

B. What the Supervisor Must Learn
A supervisor must learn to:
1. Deal with people and their differences
2. Get the job done through people
3. Recognize the problems when they exist
4. Overcome obstacles to good performance
5. Evaluate the performance of people
6. Check his own performance in terms of accomplishment

C. A Definition of Supervisor
The term supervisor means any individual having authority, in the interests of the employer, to hire, transfer, suspend, lay-off, recall, promote, discharge, assign, reward, or discipline other employees or responsibility to direct them, or to adjust their grievances, or effectively to recommend such action, if, in connection with the foregoing, exercise of such authority is not of a merely routine or clerical nature but requires the use of independent judgment.

D. Elements of the Team Concept
What is involved in teamwork? The component parts are:
1. Members
2. A leader
3. Goals
4. Plans
5. Cooperation
6. Spirit

E. Principles of Organization
1. A team member must know what his job is.
2. Be sure that the nature and scope of a job are understood.
3. Authority and responsibility should be carefully spelled out.
4. A supervisor should be permitted to make the maximum number of decisions affecting his employees.
5. Employees should report to only one supervisor.
6. A supervisor should direct only as many employees as he can handle effectively.
7. An organization plan should be flexible.

8. Inspection and performance of work should be separate.
9. Organizational problems should receive immediate attention.
10. Assign work in line with ability and experience.

F. The Four Important Parts of Every Job
1. Inherent in every job is the *accountability* for results.
2. A second set of factors in every job is *responsibilities*.
3. Along with duties and responsibilities one must have the *authority* to act within certain limits without obtaining permission to proceed.
4. No job exists in a vacuum. The supervisor is surrounded by key *relationships*.

G. Principles of Delegation
Where work is delegated for the first time, the supervisor should think in terms of these questions:
1. Who is best qualified to do this?
2. Can an employee improve his abilities by doing this?
3. How long should an employee spend on this?
4. Are there any special problems for which he will need guidance?
5. How broad a delegation can I make?

H. Principles of Effective Communications
1. Determine the media.
2. To whom directed?
3. Identification and source authority.
4. Is communication understood?

I. Principles of Work Improvement
1. Most people usually do only the work which is assigned to them.
2. Workers are likely to fit assigned work into the time available to perform it.
3. A good workload usually stimulates output.
4. People usually do their best work when they know that results will be reviewed or inspected.
5. Employees usually feel that someone else is responsible for conditions of work, workplace layout, job methods, type of tools/equipment, and other such factors.
6. Employees are usually defensive about their job security.
7. Employees have natural resistance to change.
8. Employees can support or destroy a supervisor.
9. A supervisor usually earns the respect of his people through his personal example of diligence and efficiency.

J. Areas of Job Improvement
The areas of job improvement are quite numerous, but the most common ones which a supervisor can identify and utilize are:
1. Departmental layout
2. Flow of work
3. Workplace layout
4. Utilization of manpower
5. Work methods
6. Materials handling

7. Utilization
8. Motion economy

K. Seven Key Points in Making Improvements
   1. Select the job to be improved
   2. Study how it is being done now
   3. Question the present method
   4. Determine actions to be taken
   5. Chart proposed method
   6. Get approval and apply
   7. Solicit worker participation

L. Corrective Techniques of Job Improvement
   Specific Problems
   1. Size of workload
   2. Inability to meet schedules
   3. Strain and fatigue
   4. Improper use of men and skills
   5. Waste, poor quality, unsafe conditions
   6. Bottleneck conditions that hinder output
   7. Poor utilization of equipment and machine
   8. Efficiency and productivity of labor

   General Improvement
   1. Departmental layout
   2. Flow of work
   3. Work plan layout
   4. Utilization of manpower
   5. Work methods
   6. Materials handling
   7. Utilization of equipment
   8. Motion economy

   Corrective Techniques
   1. Study with scale model
   2. Flow chart study
   3. Motion analysis
   4. Comparison of units produced to standard allowance
   5. Methods analysis
   6. Flow chart and equipment study
   7. Down time vs. running time
   8. Motion analysis

M. A Planning Checklist
   1. Objectives
   2. Controls
   3. Delegations
   4. Communications
   5. Resources
   6. Manpower

7. Equipment
8. Supplies and materials
9. Utilization of time
10. Safety
11. Money
12. Work
13. Timing of improvements

N. Five Characteristics of Good Directions
In order to get results, directions must be:
1. Possible of accomplishment
2. Agreeable with worker interests
3. Related to mission
4. Planned and complete
5. Unmistakably clear

O. Types of Directions
1. Demands or direct orders
2. Requests
3. Suggestion or implication
4. volunteering

P. Controls
A typical listing of the overall areas in which the supervisor should establish controls might be:
1. Manpower
2. Materials
3. Quality of work
4. Quantity of work
5. Time
6. Space
7. Money
8. Methods

Q. Orienting the New Employee
1. Prepare for him
2. Welcome the new employee
3. Orientation for the job
4. Follow-up

R. Checklist for Orienting New Employees   Yes   No
1. Do you appreciate the feelings of new employees
   when they first report for work?   ___   ___
2. Are you aware of the fact that the new employee must
   make a big adjustment to his job?   ___   ___
3. Have you given him good reasons for liking the job and
   the organization?   ___   ___
4. Have you prepared for his first day on the job?   ___   ___
5. Did you welcome him cordially and make him feel needed?   ___   ___

			Yes	No
6.	Did you establish rapport with him so that he feels free to talk and discuss matters with you?		___	___
7.	Did you explain his job to him and his relationship to you?		___	___
8.	Does he know that his work will be evaluated periodically on a basis that is fair and objective?		___	___
9.	Did you introduce him to his fellow workers in such a way that they are likely to accept him?		___	___
10.	Does he know what employee benefits he will receive?		___	___
11.	Does he understand the importance of being on the job and what to do if he must leave his duty station?		___	___
12.	Has he been impressed with the importance of accident prevention and safe practice?		___	___
13.	Does he generally know his way around the department?		___	___
14.	Is he under the guidance of a sponsor who will teach the right way of doing things?		___	___
15.	Do you plan to follow-up so that he will continue to adjust successfully to his job?		___	___

S. Principles of Learning
   1. Motivation
   2. Demonstration or explanation
   3. Practice

T. Causes of Poor Performance
   1. Improper training for job
   2. Wrong tools
   3. Inadequate directions
   4. Lack of supervisory follow-up
   5. Poor communications
   6. Lack of standards of performance
   7. Wrong work habits
   8. Low morale
   9. Other

U. Four Major Steps in On-The-Job Instruction
   1. Prepare the worker
   2. Present the operation
   3. Tryout performance
   4. Follow-up

V. Employees Want Five Things
   1. Security
   2 Opportunity
   3. Recognition
   4. Inclusion
   5. Expression

W. Some Don'ts in Regard to Praise
1. Don't praise a person for something he hasn't done.
2. Don't praise a person unless you can be sincere.
3. Don't be sparing in praise just because your superior withholds it from you.
4. Don't let too much time elapse between good performance and recognition of it

X. How to Gain Your Workers' Confidence
Methods of developing confidence include such things as:
1. Knowing the interests, habits, hobbies of employees
2. Admitting your own inadequacies
3. Sharing and telling of confidence in others
4. Supporting people when they are in trouble
5. Delegating matters that can be well handled
6. Being frank and straightforward about problems and working conditions
7. Encouraging others to bring their problems to you
8. Taking action on problems which impede worker progress

Y. Sources of Employee Problems
On-the-job causes might be such things as:
1. A feeling that favoritism is exercised in assignments
2. Assignment of overtime
3. An undue amount of supervision
4. Changing methods or systems
5. Stealing of ideas or trade secrets
6. Lack of interest in job
7. Threat of reduction in force
8. Ignorance or lack of communications
9. Poor equipment
10. Lack of knowing how supervisor feels toward employee
11. Shift assignments

Off-the-job problems might have to do with:
1. Health
2. Finances
3. Housing
4. Family

Z. The Supervisor's Key to Discipline
There are several key points about discipline which the supervisor should keep in mind:
1. Job discipline is one of the disciplines of life and is directed by the supervisor.
2. It is more important to correct an employee fault than to fix blame for it.
3. Employee performance is affected by problems both on the job and off.
4. Sudden or abrupt changes in behavior can be indications of important employee problems.
5. Problems should be dealt with as soon as possible after they are identified.
6. The attitude of the supervisor may have more to do with solving problems than the techniques of problem solving.
7. Correction of employee behavior should be resorted to only after the supervisor is sure that training or counseling will not be helpful.

8. Be sure to document your disciplinary actions.
9. Make sure that you are disciplining on the basis of facts rather than personal feelings.
10. Take each disciplinary step in order, being careful not to make snap judgments, or decisions based on impatience.

AA. Five Important Processes of Management
1. Planning
2. Organizing
3. Scheduling
4. Controlling
5. Motivating

BB. When the Supervisor Fails to Plan
1. Supervisor creates impression of not knowing his job
2. May lead to excessive overtime
3. Job runs itself—supervisor lacks control
4. Deadlines and appointments missed
5. Parts of the work go undone
6. Work interrupted by emergencies
7. Sets a bad example
8. Uneven workload creates peaks and valleys
9. Too much time on minor details at expense of more important tasks

CC. Fourteen General Principles of Management
1. Division of work
2. Authority and responsibility
3. Discipline
4. Unity of command
5. Unity of direction
6. Subordination of individual interest to general interest
7. Remuneration of personnel
8. Centralization
9. Scalar chain
10. Order
11. Equity
12. Stability of tenure of personnel
13. Initiative
14. Esprit de corps

DD. Change

Bringing about change is perhaps attempted more often, and yet less well understood, than anything else the supervisor does. How do people generally react to change? (People tend to resist change that is imposed upon them by other individuals or circumstances.

Change is characteristic of every situation. It is a part of every real endeavor where the efforts of people are concerned.

1. Why do people resist change?
   People may resist change because of:
   a. Fear of the unknown
   b. Implied criticism
   c. Unpleasant experiences in the past
   d. Fear of loss of status
   e. Threat to the ego
   f. Fear of loss of economic stability

2. How can we best overcome the resistance to change?
   In initiating change, take these steps:
   a. Get ready to sell
   b. Identify sources of help
   c. Anticipate objections
   d. Sell benefits
   e. Listen in depth
   f. Follow up

II. Brief Topical Summaries

   A. Who/What is the Supervisor?
      1. The supervisor is often called the "highest level employee and the lowest level manager."
      2. A supervisor is a member of both management and the work group. He acts as a bridge between the two.
      3. Most problems in supervision are in the area of human relations, or people problems.
      4. Employees expect: Respect, opportunity to learn and to advance, and a sense of belonging, and so forth.
      5. Supervisors are responsible for directing people and organizing work. Planning is of paramount importance.
      6. A position description is a set of duties and responsibilities inherent to a given position.
      7. It is important to keep the position description up-to-date and to provide each employee with his own copy.

   B. The Sociology of Work
      1. People are alike in many ways; however, each individual is unique.
      2. The supervisor is challenged in getting to know employee differences. Acquiring skills in evaluating individuals is an asset.
      3. Maintaining meaningful working relationships in the organization is of great importance.
      4. The supervisor has an obligation to help individuals to develop to their fullest potential.
      5. Job rotation on a planned basis helps to build versatility and to maintain interest and enthusiasm in work groups.
      6. Cross training (job rotation) provides backup skills.

7. The supervisor can help reduce tension by maintaining a sense of humor, providing guidance to employees, and by making reasonable and timely decisions. Employees respond favorably to working under reasonably predictable circumstances.
8. Change is characteristic of all managerial behavior. The supervisor must adjust to changes in procedures, new methods, technological changes, and to a number of new and sometimes challenging situations.
9. To overcome the natural tendency for people to resist change, the supervisor should become more skillful in initiating change.

C. Principles and Practices of Supervision
1. Employees should be required to answer to only one superior.
2. A supervisor can effectively direct only a limited number of employees, depending upon the complexity, variety, and proximity of the jobs involved.
3. The organizational chart presents the organization in graphic form. It reflects lines of authority and responsibility as well as interrelationships of units within the organization.
4. Distribution of work can be improved through an analysis using the "Work Distribution Chart."
5. The "Work Distribution Chart" reflects the division of work within a unit in understandable form.
6. When related tasks are given to an employee, he has a better chance of increasing his skills through training.
7. The individual who is given the responsibility for tasks must also be given the appropriate authority to insure adequate results.
8. The supervisor should delegate repetitive, routine work. Preparation of recurring reports, maintaining leave and attendance records are some examples.
9. Good discipline is essential to good task performance. Discipline is reflected in the actions of employees on the job in the absence of supervision.
10. Disciplinary action may have to be taken when the positive aspects of discipline have failed. Reprimand, warning, and suspension are examples of disciplinary action.
11. If a situation calls for a reprimand, be sure it is deserved and remember it is to be done in private.

D. Dynamic Leadership
1. A style is a personal method or manner of exerting influence.
2. Authoritarian leaders often see themselves as the source of power and authority.
3. The democratic leader often perceives the group as the source of authority and power.
4. Supervisors tend to do better when using the pattern of leadership that is most natural for them.
5. Social scientists suggest that the effective supervisor use the leadership style that best fits the problem or circumstances involved.
6. All four styles—telling, selling, consulting, joining—have their place. Using one does not preclude using the other at another time.

7. The theory X point of view assumes that the average person dislikes work, will avoid it whenever possible, and must be coerced to achieve organizational objectives.
8. The theory Y point of view assumes that the average person considers work to be a natural as play, and, when the individual is committed, he requires little supervision or direction to accomplish desired objectives.
9. The leader's basic assumptions concerning human behavior and human nature affect his actions, decisions, and other managerial practices.
10. Dissatisfaction among employees is often present, but difficult to isolate. The supervisor should seek to weaken dissatisfaction by keeping promises, being sincere and considerate, keeping employees informed, and so forth.
11. Constructive suggestions should be encouraged during the natural progress of the work.

E. Processes for Solving Problems
1. People find their daily tasks more meaningful and satisfying when they can improve them.
2. The causes of problems, or the key factors, are often hidden in the background. Ability to solve problems often involves the ability to isolate them from their backgrounds. There is some substance to the cliché that some persons "can't see the forest for the trees."
3. New procedures are often developed from old ones. Problems should be broken down into manageable parts. New ideas can be adapted from old one.
4. People think differently in problem-solving situations. Using a logical, patterned approach is often useful. One approach found to be useful includes these steps:
   a. Define the problem
   b. Establish objectives
   c. Get the facts
   d. Weigh and decide
   e. Take action
   f. Evaluate action

F. Training for Results
1. Participants respond best when they feel training is important to them.
2. The supervisor has responsibility for the training and development of those who report to him.
3. When training is delegated to others, great care must be exercised to insure the trainer has knowledge, aptitude, and interest for his work as a trainer.
4. Training (learning) of some type goes on continually. The most successful supervisor makes certain the learning contributes in a productive manner to operational goals.
5. New employees are particularly susceptible to training. Older employees facing new job situations require specific training, as well as having need for development and growth opportunities.
6. Training needs require continuous monitoring.
7. The training officer of an agency is a professional with a responsibility to assist supervisors in solving training problems.

8. Many of the self-development steps important to the supervisor's own growth are equally important to the development of peers and subordinates. Knowledge of these is important when the supervisor consults with others on development and growth opportunities.

G. Health, Safety, and Accident Prevention
1. Management-minded supervisors take appropriate measures to assist employees in maintaining health and in assuring safe practices in the work environment.
2. Effective safety training and practices help to avoid injury and accidents.
3. Safety should be a management goal. All infractions of safety which are observed should be corrected without exception.
4. Employees' safety attitude, training and instruction, provision of safe tools and equipment, supervision, and leadership are considered highly important factors which contribute to safety and which can be influenced directly by supervisors.
5. When accidents do occur, they should be investigated promptly for very important reasons, including the fact that information which is gained can be used to prevent accidents in the future.

H. Equal Employment Opportunity
1. The supervisor should endeavor to treat all employees fairly, without regard to religion, race, sex, or national origin.
2. Groups tend to reflect the attitude of the leader. Prejudice can be detected even in very subtle form. Supervisors must strive to create a feeling of mutual respect and confidence in every employee.
3. Complete utilization of all human resources is a national goal. Equitable consideration should be accorded women in the work force, minority-group members, the physically and mentally handicapped, and the older employee. The important question is: "Who can do the job?"
4. Training opportunities, recognition for performance, overtime assignments, promotional opportunities, and all other personnel actions are to be handled on an equitable basis.

I. Improving Communications
1. Communications is achieving understanding between the sender and the receiver of a message. It also means sharing information—the creation of understanding.
2. Communication is basic to all human activity. Words are means of conveying meanings; however, real meanings are in people.
3. There are very practical differences in the effectiveness of one-way, impersonal, and two-way communications. Words spoken face-to-face are better understood. Telephone conversations are effective, but lack the rapport of person-to-person exchanges. The whole person communicates.
4. Cooperation and communication in an organization go hand in hand. When there is a mutual respect between people, spelling out rules and procedures for communicating is unnecessary.
5. There are several barriers to effective communications. These include failure to listen with respect and understanding, lack of skill in feedback, and misinterpreting the meanings of words used by the speaker. It is also common

practice to listen to what we want to hear, and tune out things we do not want to hear.
6. Communication is management's chief problem. The supervisor should accept the challenge to communicate more effectively and to improve interagency and intra-agency communications.
7. The supervisor may often plan for and conduct meetings. The planning phase is critical and may determine the success or the failure of a meeting.
8. Speaking before groups usually requires extra effort. Stage fright may never disappear completely, but it can be controlled.

J. Self-Development
1. Every employee is responsible for his own self-development.
2. Toastmaster and toastmistress clubs offer opportunities to improve skills in oral communications.
3. Planning for one's own self-development is of vital importance. Supervisors know their own strengths and limitations better than anyone else.
4. Many opportunities are open to aid the supervisor in his developmental efforts, including job assignments; training opportunities, both governmental and non-governmental—to include universities and professional conferences and seminars.
5. Programmed instruction offers a means of studying at one's own rate.
6. Where difficulties may arise from a supervisor's being away from his work for training, he may participate in televised home study or correspondence courses to meet his self-development needs.

K. Teaching and Training
1. The Teaching Process
Teaching is encouraging and guiding the learning activities of students toward established goals. In most cases this process consists of five steps: preparation, presentation, summarization, evaluation, and application.

  a. Preparation
  Preparation is two-fold in nature; that of the supervisor and the employee. Preparation by the supervisor is absolutely essential to success. He must know what, when, where, how, and whom he will teach. Some of the factors that should be considered are:
  1) The objectives
  2) The materials needed
  3) The methods to be used
  4) Employee participation
  5) Employee interest
  6) Training aids
  7) Evaluation
  8) Summarization

  Employee preparation consists in preparing the employee to receive the material. Probably the most important single factor in the preparation of the employee is arousing and maintaining his interest. He must know the objectives of the training, why he is there, how the material can be used, and its importance to him.

b. Presentation
In presentation, have a carefully designed plan and follow it. The plan should be accurate and complete, yet flexible enough to meet situations as they arise. The method of presentation will be determined by the particular situation and objectives.

c. Summary
A summary should be made at the end of every training unit and program. In addition, there may be internal summaries depending on the nature of the material being taught. The important thing is that the trainee must always be able to understand how each part of the new material relates to the whole.

d. Application
The supervisor must arrange work so the employee will be given a chance to apply new knowledge or skills while the material is still clear in his mind and interest is high. The trainee does not really know whether he has learned the material until he has been given a chance to apply it. If the material is not applied, it loses most of its value.

e. Evaluation
The purpose of all training is to promote learning. To determine whether the training has been a success or failure, the supervisor must evaluate this learning.
In the broadest sense, evaluation includes all the devices, methods, skills, and techniques used by the supervisor to keep himself and the employees informed as to their progress toward the objectives they are pursuing. The extent to which the employee has mastered the knowledge, skills, and abilities, or changed his attitudes, as determined by the program objectives, is the extent to which instruction has succeeded or failed.
Evaluation should not be confined to the end of the lesson, day, or program but should be used continuously. We shall note later the way this relates to the rest of the teaching process.

2. Teaching Methods
A teaching method is a pattern of identifiable student and instructor activity used in presenting training material.
All supervisors are faced with the problem of deciding which method should be used at a given time.

a. Lecture
The lecture is direct oral presentation of material by the supervisor. The present trend is to place less emphasis on the trainer's activity and more on that of the trainee.

b. Discussion
Teaching by discussion or conference involves using questions and other techniques to arouse interest and focus attention upon certain areas, and by doing so creating a learning situation. This can be one of the most

valuable methods because it gives the employees an opportunity to express their ideas and pool their knowledge.

    c. Demonstration

The demonstration is used to teach how something works or how to do something. It can be used to show a principle or what the results of a series of actions will be. A well-staged demonstration is particularly effective because it shows proper methods of performance in a realistic manner.

    d. Performance

Performance is one of the most fundamental of all learning techniques or teaching methods. The trainee may be able to tell how a specific operation should be performed but he cannot be sure he knows how to perform the operation until he has done so.

As with all methods, there are certain advantages and disadvantages to each method.

    e. Which Method to Use

Moreover, there are other methods and techniques of teaching. It is difficult to use any method without other methods entering into it. In any learning situation, a combination of methods is usually more effective than any one method alone.

Finally, evaluation must be integrated into the other aspects of the teaching-learning process.

It must be used in the motivation of the trainees; it must be used to assist in developing understanding during the training; and it must be related to employee application of the results of training.

This is distinctly the role of the supervisor.

www.ingramcontent.com/pod-product-compliance
Lightning Source LLC
Chambersburg PA
CBHW081824300426
44116CB00014B/2476